CLOSE CALLS

For
Frans + Di
with affection
and happy memories
of the cruise
we shared!
JR

CLOSE CALLS

*The World's First
Unauthorized Autobiography*

Jeremiah Reedy, S.T.B., M.A.,[2] Ph.D.

To order additional copies of this book, contact:
Xlibris Corporation
1-888-795-4274
www.Xlibris.com
Orders@Xlibris.com
72175

CONTENTS

Dedication

In memory of our Irish ancestors who, to escape starvation and oppression, left their families and beloved homeland, crossed the Atlantic in "coffin ships," made their way to the Midwest where they survived blizzards, droughts, dust storms, economic depression, poverty, and even persecution to lay the foundations for our lives of comfort, prosperity, and service, lives beyond their wildest dreams.

PREFACE

What is there to love
that I have not loved?

Wallace Stevens

The unexamined life isn't worth
living.

Socrates

The title of these memoirs may suggest that I wrote them against my will. That would be only half right. A part of me wanted to write an account of my life, and another part of me opposed doing so. In the end I overcame my misgivings and went ahead. I realize that writing one's memoirs may sound pretentious since it used to be that only important people such as former presidents and retired diplomats did so. This is no longer the case; there are now "kids" of twenty-five who are writing memoirs.

There are several advantages in recording one's memoirs instead of writing history. For one thing readers can always criticize the historian if they find errors of fact. The memoirist is, however, incorrigible (in the original, Latin sense of the word) since no one can say, "That's not how you remember that event." Another advantage is that it doesn't require a lot of research. I have written fifteen-page "scholarly articles" that have sixty-five footnotes. I've sometimes read whole books just to support one sentence with one footnote. For a long time I've thought how much fun it would be to write something that wouldn't require months of research, and it was fun. Anyone who relaxes, closes his eyes and travels back in time will be astounded to discover how much is stored deep down in the recesses of the mind. I made outlines and drafts full of abbreviations, and then I dictated to my computer using MacSpeech Dictate. It's wonderful to speak and see the words appear on the screen. Of course, the first draft required extensive editing for many reasons, but I enjoyed that too. In a sense I only did what grandparents have done since tape recorders were invented, but now technology enables us to turn it into a book. The bare bones, non-scintillating style of what I have produced is partially due to the fact that it was dictated. I could have spent months or even years polishing what I have written, but as the poet Andrew Marvell put it, "At my back I always hear/Time's winged chariot hurrying near . . ."

I mainly have my grandchildren in mind as an audience, but it may be that other relatives and even some friends will find the end product diverting. I have no illusions about any widespread interest, and I certainly don't expect to sell any copies or earn any royalties.

If there is a pattern to my life, it is that Divine Providence repeatedly saved me from my own foolishness. Time and again I wanted something desperately and didn't get it, only to find that God had something much better in store for me. There were many more "close calls" than I discuss herein—many too frightening to contemplate or record. Looking at what I've accomplished in another way, a cynical friend once told me I haven't done as well as my friends expected, but I've done better than my enemies hoped! There is much to be thankful for.

My teacher, Elizabeth Jarrett Andrew, read a draft of the manuscript and made many valuable suggestions. It is a pleasure to thank her publicly for her assistance and inspiration.

CHAPTER I

THE REEDYS OF BERESFORD

It is indeed desirable to be well descended,
but the glory belongs to our ancestors.
Plutarch

According to Isabel (Reedy) Sattler, author of *The Reedy Family of Union County, Dakota Territory*, my great-grandfather, John Reedy (1815-55) and his wife Hanora (O'Brien) Reedy (1818-1862) immigrated from Limerick, Ireland to the U.S. and settled in Stephenson County, Illinois in 184. They were the parents of seven children: James (1843-1916), Mary (1844-1882), Patrick (1845-1909), Catherine (1847-1887), Richard (1849-19030), John W. (1850-1934) (known as J.W.), and the youngest, Jeremiah (known as Jere or Jerre), my grandfather (1853-1900). J.W. and Jeremiah moved from Illinois to Fountain in south eastern Minnesota where they ran a hardware store known as "J.W. Reedy & Bro." "In May of 1877 they transported by train 150 cattle from Fountain to Le Mars, Iowa, the end of the line. From there they drove them overland to what would be the site of Beresford, a cattle drive of perhaps thirty-five miles."

(Digression: If anyone is wondering why the Irish were leaving Ireland at this time, I can recommend Cecil Woodham-Smith's *The Great Hunger: Ireland 1845-9* (published in 1962). This book was first recommended to me by Cousin Denis O'Connor during a visit to Ballyferriter. He said that, although she was English, she had written the best book to date on the "potato famine." The western counties of Ireland were hardest hit, which included Kerry Co. where both the Reedys and the O'Connors lived. Woodham-Smith agreed with work done earlier by John Mitchel (1815-75) who argued that the "British government committed genocide against the Irish people." Benjamin Jowett of Oxford (a famous classicist and translator of Plato) reports an attitude which, I fear, was all too common.

He says, "I have always felt a certain horror of political economists since I heard one of them say that the famine in Ireland would not kill more than a million people, and that would scarcely be enough to do much good." Between 1846 and 1851 Ireland's population fell by *ca.* 25% to 6,000,000. One million died of starvation and disease, and more emigrated. For a discussion of historians who disagree with Woodham-Smith see *The Great Potato Famine* by James Donnelly. End of digression)

In those days it was the railroad that could make or break a town, and a number of communities were hoping to be designated a depot, but the Chicago and Northwestern chose a stagecoach stop known as "Paris," and renamed it Beresford for Lord Charles Beresford, an admiral in the British navy and major stock holder of the railroad. Jere Reedy and his nephew J.L. opened the first hardware store in Beresford and called it "J. Reedy & Co." (Jere had been an "apprentice tinner" in Minnesota.) In 1880 Jere married Mary Elizabeth O'Reilly who was born in Smiths Falls, Ontario on July 22, 1865. She was fifteen at the time of their marriage. "Mary Liz," as she was called, was our grandmother and lived with us for approximately nine years before she passed away on August 14, 1953. Jere and Mary Liz had four children Mary (Mamie), Katherine, Loretta, who died at age one, and John Ernest (J.E.) my dad. Jere was struck by lightning and killed in 1900 at the age of 46. His obituary states that Jere and his brother J.W. had been "almost constantly connected in business from their boyhood up" and "were bound together by the closest ties and the best and friendliest feeling[s] . . ." (Sattler, p. 127)

The following piece about J.W. from a "turn-of-the century biographical record of prominent citizens" provided by Mrs. Sattler is worth quoting at length:

> John W. Reedy, one of the most prominent men of Beresford, near where he is carrying on an extensive farming and stock business, is one of the wide-awake and wealthy citizens of the Union County. He is a fine type of our self-made men, having begun for himself with absolutely nothing except the tools which nature gave him. From his first employment at a salary of $12 per month he has steadily risen by his own efforts on the ladder of Fortune and is now possessed of a very comfortable competence.
>
> Mr. Reedy is yet in the prime of life, having been born October 9, 1850 in Stephenson County, Illinois. His parents John and

Hanora (O'Brien) Reedy were early settlers of the Prairie State where their deaths occurred. Our subject was but four years old when his father passed from time to eternity, and when twelve was deprived of a mother's watchfulness and care. Thus early in life he was thrown on his own resources and for this reason his success is all the more remarkable. Until eighteen years of age he continued to make his home in Stephenson County, Illinois receiving his education in the common schools there and completing it with a term in the La Crosse Business College. He worked for others from the time he was twelve years old until he had finished his schooling and then started in the hardware business in Fountain, Minnesota where he remained for three years. In May, 1877 he came to Dakota territory and settled on a farm in Prairie Township. For eight years he continued to make his home on this farm and then when the town of Beresford was located, he removed to there. His dwelling was the first one built in the town and was erected on the first resident lot sold. He then began the breeding, buying and shipping of livestock and now has some fine specimens of purebred cattle. He first devoted his time to the breeding of Durham cattle exclusively, but on March 27, 1895 he purchased twenty-five head of polled Aberdeen-Angus cattle, the ancestors of which were imported from Scotland and has since paid strict attention to improving his herd of this breed. The animals are all registered. At the head of the herd is Heatherlad of Emerson who, when two years and three months old weighed 1850 pounds. This animal was calved October 17, 1892, and is sired by Imp Jim Jams, dam Rosa Bonhuer of Turlington. Then he has Bessie of North Oak, Bess of Cottage Grove, Tina of Cottage Grove, Judges' Pride and Ideal of Cottage Grove II. The balance of the herd are all of the same strain and mostly sired by Guido Knight, the sire of the heifer Nell Gwynn that took first premium at the World's Fair at Chicago in 1893. Some of the herd are also of the get of Blackbird King and includes Ranter, Claire Duff and Napoleon. The herd now consists of thirty-five head of choice animals, Mr. Reedy having disposed of six head of young males. He is also an extensive handler and breeder of hogs and has some fine specimens of Poland China swine on his farm. Among his horses he has the imported English hackney "Stuntney Movement,"

registered in the English Hackney Stud Book volume 9. This
magnificent piece of horseflesh was foaled in 1889, is a dark
brown in color, and is sired by Clockwork, dam Beauty. He
was bred by Colonel Ambrose Stuntney Hall of England, and
is the finest representative of the equine species in the county.
He stands seventeen hands high, weighs 1500 pounds, possesses
high knee action and is an extremely good performer. For mares
Mr. Reedy has Lattie Collins, registered in volume 12 and
various others, the get of noted sire;s in all he has twenty-two
brood mares Mr. Reedy is also one of the largest land owners of
Union County, his farmlands footing up an area of 1,760 acres,
and besides this he is also the possessor of fifty acres of town
property. He rents a large part of the land. Politically he has
always used his elective franchise in the support of candidates
nominated by the Democratic Party and has taken an active
interest in local matters. He is now president of the Beresford
town council Mr. Reedy was married in 1876 to Ms. Johanna
Murphy, a native of Michigan. They have no children of their
own but are raising a young lady, Miss Theresa Ryan, a niece of
our subject. The family are all members of the Catholic Church
and devout in their religious beliefs. (109-110)

As Mrs. Sattler observes, J.W. who had no children devotes considerable
space to the blood lines of his livestock! Another interesting fact re J.W.:
He seems always to have had in-laws living with him; his first wife's niece
and mother lived with them, and his second wife, Pauline, brought her
bachelor brother, Carl, with her to the Reedy home.

One of J.W.'s side-lines was auctioneering, and he came to be known
as "Colonel Reedy." He seems to have specialized in selling land, and in
his best single day he sold 7,000 acres of school land near Elk Point for
much more than the expected price. He also conducted sales in "at least
twenty states" and two Canadian provinces. One wonders how a person
became an auctioneer in the late 19th century. Were there apprenticeships,
or did a person simply observe others and plunge into it? (Auctions are
quite ancient. The fifth century B.C. Greek historian Herodotus says that
the Babylonians auctioned women off for marriage. Among the Romans
auctions were very common, but after the fall of the Roman empire nothing
is heard about them until they came into favor in 17th century England.
Whether or not they were common in Ireland in the 19th century is hard to

say. On the one hand, the Irish didn't have many possessions to sell; on the other hand, foreclosures were common.)

J.W. was also a traveler. He traveled in "every state of the Union" (in 1890 there were forty-four states in the U.S.), in Alberta, Saskatchewan, British Columbia, and the Bahamas. In 1912 he traveled for two months in Europe, visiting among other places Limerick, Ireland where he failed to locate any relatives. (If he couldn't find them in those days, it's not surprising that we can't find Reedy relatives in Ireland today!) The fact that J.W. return to Ireland at all is remarkable and a vivid proof of his wealth and success. Our O'Connor relatives in Ireland told me that, when young people bade their parents farewell and left home for America in the 19th century, they were almost never reunited.

J.W. was well connected in some circles in Chicago. Mrs. Sattler included in her history the following letter to J.W. from Mr. H. J. Wagen, Division Freight and Passenger Agent, Chicago and North Western Railroad Company Traffic Department, Winona, Minnesota. It was found among the papers of J.W.'s widow, Pauline, when she died in her nineties in California in 1980.

June 18, 1928

Dear Mr. Reedy

The Chicago and North Western Employees band are to play at the State American Legion Convention in Aberdeen Friday, July 13 and Saturday, July 14. We can route them via Hawarden and can start them out a day earlier so as to stop in Beresdord if you think you would like to have the band for an afternoon and evening concert on Wednesday, July 11, arriving there on train number 23 at 2:00 PM.

What would you say to making a "Reedy Day" of it, or maybe you could arrange for some community affair in the afternoon and band concert in the evening. They will leave there the following morning on train number 1 so you would have the use of the band in the afternoon and evening. Perhaps we could get the Governor to come down and make it a big affair at Beresford for not only your citizens but those of the adjacent towns.

There will be no expense as the Band travels at their own in their own sleepers, and we will pay for our own meals while at

Beresford. Of course it is needless for us to tell to tell you what a wonderful band we have as you have heard them. There are about fifty pieces in the band now.

You have always been so kind in helping out and cooperating with the C and NW in every way that we could like to reciprocate in this manner. Would be glad to hear from you as to what you think of a program of this kind, and if it meets with your approval, I shall be glad to come down and make all preliminary arrangements so we can get out special advertising etc.

I'm sorry indeed I missed you while the Sioux City Jobbers visited Beresford, but I was unable to locate you anywhere. If you will kindly let me know as soon as possible, we will go ahead and perfect the arrangements

Kindest personal regards and best wishes

Sincerely
H.J. Wagen

The Beresford *Republic* reports that the concerts did indeed take place, and they were in honor of Col. J.W. Reedy who was a friend of the president and vice-president of the railroad. Following the afternoon concert there was a ball game, and at 6:30 members of the band were served supper in the Legion Hall. The evening concert lasted from 7:30 to 9:00. Dignitaries were entertained at the Reedy residence.

What J.W. accomplished was extraordinary, especially for someone who was an orphan at twelve, and at a time when most farmers had forty acres. (That land today (2008) would be worth from $3000 to $5000 per acre. 1760 x $3000 = $5,280,000; 1760 x $5000 = $8,800,000. If J.W.'s wealth had stayed in the family, the Reedys could have been one of the most prominent families in southeastern South Dakota.) Mrs. Sattler also reports that, although J.W. was never in politics, he was an active member of the Democratic Party and was well known in Democratic circles. Pauline, on the other hand, his second wife, was or became a conservative and left a "large bequest" to the far-right John Birch Society. Mrs. Sattler describes Pauline at the time of her death as "wealthy."

J.W., who at one time owned a herd of 300 registered cattle, was a charter member of an organization that sponsored the International Livestock Exposition in Chicago which became the most famous show of that sort in North America. He was the "fourth man to contribute $100 toward the development" of the organization. (Sattler, p. 116)

My folks didn't reminisce much, but I do remember Dad saying that, when his wife was ill, J.W. had a doctor come from Chicago to Sioux City by train, and then J.W. chartered a train from Sioux City to Beresford. While the doctor was examining his wife, the train crew ate a meal in the kitchen. Then the train was turned around and headed back to Sioux City.

J.W. lost his wife Johanna to cancer in 1914, and a year later he went to Chicago to the "Kimball people" and ordered the largest pipe organ available (610 pipes). It was installed in the Catholic Church in Beresford in memory of Johanna Reedy. Three years later J.W. married Pauline Seegar, who was about forty years younger than he was (he was 68 and she about 28). She had been hired to take care of his late wife. Pauline's brother Carl Seegar moved to Beresford from Youngstown, Ohio and became the principal and Latin teacher of the local high school. Though a Protestant, he became the official organist at the Catholic Church.

Dad who almost never talked about J.W. did say once that J.W. had owned one of the first cars in South Dakota. It was a White Steamer. Later he bought a custom built Packard which had been made for a wealthy person in Omaha who decided he didn't want it. In newspaper accounts of J.W.'s activities that I've read automobiles are never mentioned. (I paid the S.D. Historian a modest fee to search state records for autos owned by J.W., but they failed to find any listed. I was told, however, that he could have owned cars before license plates were required!)

I have dwelt on the Reedys in Beresford at considerable length because I think that understanding what their life was like before the Great Depression will explain much of what happened to our family after 1929. (Details on this in the next chapter.) My theory is predicated on the following points:

1. There was a special relationship between J.W. and Dad's dad, Jere. They were "inseparable."
2. J.W. knew what it was like to be fatherless, having lost his own father at age four (and his mother at age twelve).
3. J.W. had no children and would have looked upon Dad as his own son after Jere was killed by lightning.
4. Dad hoped to follow in J.W.'s footsteps, to be another J.W., perhaps even to surpass him since Dad had a college degree with a major in "Agriculture." (He took courses *inter alia* in Farm Crops, Stock Judging, Diseases of animals, Veterinary Hygiene, Breeds of

Live Stock, Poultry Breeding, Horticulture, Entomology, Rural Sociology, Soils, Economics and Agricultural Economics, etc. plus General Botany, Chemistry, Physics, Spanish and typing.)

5. Dad's hopes were dashed by two events: J.W.'s marriage to Pauline Seegar in 1918 and the Great Depression which started in 1929. The fact that Pauline was forty years younger than J.W. meant that she would most likely outlive him for many years. Any money Dad might inherit from J.W. wouldn't come for years. In addition the Depression had a devastating effect on farmers in South Dakota. Crops were left to rot in the fields since harvesting them would have cost more than they were worth. Stress caused by economic conditions after 1929 brought on Dad's "hay fever" which led him to abandon farming and move to western South Dakota. Unemployment, poverty and hopelessness caused him to turn to drinking as an escape. The Depression affected Dad in ways it didn't affect others (e.g. Mom's brothers) because Dad had seen and experience what life could be like, as exemplified by J.W. before the Depression. (J.W. died in 1934. Evidently the market crash did not affect him seriously. If it had, Pauline would not have left a "considerable fortune" when she died in 1980. Mom took us to visit Pauline a few times when I was in grade school, and Pauline lived in the Reedy residence in Beresford. Three things struck me: how big and beautiful her house was, she had a parrot, and she always gave us kids money!)

Another distinguished relative (by marriage) from Beresford's pioneer period is William J. Bulow. Born in 1869, he grew up in Moscow, Ohio and earned his law degree at the University of Michigan in Ann Arbor. According to Mrs. Sattler, "He opened a law practice in Beresford and contributed his many talents to the development of the town, serving as mayor, city attorney, and judge of Union County . . ." (Why he chose to settle in Beresford isn't explained.) In 1898 he married Katherine Reedy, daughter of James Reedy and, therefore, niece of J.W. Reedy. Bulow later served two terms as Governor of South Dakota (1927-31). (He was the first Democrat elected to that office.) He served two terms in the U.S. Senate (1931-43), but was defeated for a third term by Tom Berry, also a former S.D. Governor. Bulow had been critical of some New Deal programs and lost the support of F.D.R. (He had accused the W.P.A. of paying men to dig holes and then fill them in.) Bulow lived in D.C. until his death in

1960. While visiting Aunt Mamie and Cousin Eileen in D.C. in 1954 or 1955 they introduced me to Bulow, and we spent a pleasant afternoon with him.

In two articles from the *Saturday Evening Post* which I saved for many years, Bulow described how he entertained President Coolidge ("When Cal Coolidge Came to Visit Us" Jan. 4, 1947) and how he dealt with Gutzon Borglum, the sculptor of Mt. Rushmore ("My Days with Gutzon Borglum" Jan. 11, 1947). These articles were described as two chapters from Bulow's autobiography which, as far as I know, was never published. In the first one the Governor related how he had to threaten the highway commissioner to get the road from Hermosa to the State Game Lodge graveled so Coolidge could travel to and from Rapid City. When Coolidge visited Pierre and Bulow was giving him a tour of the city, the President asked if there was much moonshine being made in town. The Governor didn't know if he was checking up on them or if he wanted a drink. Bulow considered Borglum a great sculptor, but impossible to get along with and as a fund raiser and diplomat, among the very worst.

When Bulow died, an obituary in *Time* said that he had entered the race for the Senate "with great expectorations" which meant, I assume, that he chewed tobacco.

One branch of the Reedy clan *ca.* 1900

J.W. Reedy   Mom and Donna *ca.* 1926

CHAPTER II

FROM WOMB TO SIXTH GRADE

> God could not be everywhere,
> and therefore He made mothers.
> Jewish proverb

I was born on May 17, 1934 in Rapid City, South Dakota five years into the Great Depression. According to my birth certificate Dad was a "wool buyer" and had been for two years although I am not sure what that entailed. Mom and Dad were married on February 5, 1925 in St. Agnes Church, Vermillion, by Fr. Flood during the 7:00 a.m. Mass. In an account of the wedding I found in Gramma's scrapbook, Dad was described as a "progressive young farmer and stock raiser" who was a local "live wire, well known to all." Mom and Dad met while she was teaching "at Emmet." (She had attended U.S.D. for two years and earned a teacher's certificate.) After a honeymoon in the Twin Cities, they moved to the Reedy farm north of Beresford.

Donna, the oldest of us four kids, was born in Beresford on December 30, 1925. She passed away on December 21, 1978 at the age of 52. Joe was born on August 23, 1927 in Midland, South Dakota, a town that had a population of 179 in 2000 and 152 in 2006. According to Joe, Dad gave up farming because of "hay fever" and moved the family to Midland where the climate was said to be more salubrious. Between Joe and me there is a hiatus of seven years which, as far as I know, the folks never explained. (We were not the sort of family that discussed such matters.) Carol was born on December 1, 1935. Our family was in some sense two families since Donna was in high school when Carol was born.

Mom told me that I was such a crabby baby in the hospital that the nurses suggested they call me "Jeremiah" after the local bishop who was apparently something of a curmudgeon. Jeremiah was, however, a family name among the Reedys. (As a kid I hated the name, but when I took Hebrew years later at St. Bonaventure's, I was the "teacher's pet." At Macalester during the early 1970s I became famous for my "jeremiads.")

My earliest memories are of my Dad coming home drunk in the middle of the night and arguing with Mom downstairs in the kitchen. There would be pounding on the table and chairs scraping the floor. Usually the argument was about money or the use of the car. I was terrified for fear he would hurt Mom. According to Gramma Reedy drinking became a major problem for my Dad when J.W. died in 1934 and left all his money to his young wife Pauline. Dad had expected a share of J.W.'s sizable fortune. Dad was what is called a binge drinker. He would go two weeks or so without a drop, and then on pay day he would vanish only to show up sometimes a day or two later "totally wasted." In the 1930s and 1940s, at least among Irish Catholics, alcoholism was seen mostly as a sin, confession being presumably the solution. (Taking "the oath" not to drink was a common practice among Irish immigrants. Mom's brother Jack took it, and he told me once he had never so much as tasted beer.) Dad was thought of as a "party boy" whose drinking bouts were considered "parties." Actually I would say he was about as far from being a party boy as one could get. Far from being someone who just loved a good time, I now see him as a profoundly disturbed and emotionally sick individual. Dad could not express any feelings unless he was drinking—not love or anger or appreciation or anything else. I assume that the feelings would build up for a week or two until the pressure became unbearable. It's odd that no one suspected that addiction was something other than a sin in the '40s or '50s, but it is not easy to "think outside the box." While I am not one to give the field of psychology much credit for anything, I suppose psychologists deserve some credit for the change in attitude towards alcoholism and other forms of addiction. After the folks got TV, Mom used to watch Bishop Sheen who said in one of his programs that alcoholism was a disease. Mom told me this, and I think it gave her some piece of mind.

South Dakota was hit hard by the Great Depression which began in 1929, and in addition there was the drought and the resulting dust storms. Dad was frequently unemployed, and I assume that being without a job and income and having a family to support must have caused almost unbearable anxiety, so unbearable that one would do practically anything for relief. Alcohol alone seems to have brought him some relief. Having suffered from acute anxiety two or three times in my life, I have some idea how terrible it can be. I used to read poetry and listen to classical music for relief. I also took up yoga which helped, as did meditation, and at one point I joined a support group called "Living with Cancer." I began writing my memoirs. Most importantly I had my faith. (Fortunately in my case drinking did nothing to relieve the misery.) Dad had none of these having left the Church some years earlier.

Dad, as I said was frequently unemployed, and he lost at least one good job because of his drinking. This was certainly the cause of something else I recall from the preschool years. We moved frequently. Poor Mom was often out looking for an apartment. I remember living in a basement apartment, and when I was in the first grade we lived upstairs in a house where the landlord who was a wood carver lived on the main floor. We also lived outside Rapid City in a town called Phillip, in another town called Dupree, and then in Gregory and Winner. The population of Philip in 2000 was 885. Dupree had a population of 434 in 2000. In 2007 the population of Gregory was 1,193, and the estimated median value of houses was $37,700. Winner's population in the same year was 2,007 with an estimated median value of houses being $60,400. Both Philip and Dupree were county seats of their respective counties. Most likely we moved to these places when Dad was working for the Farm Security Administration, one of Roosevelt's New Deal programs, the mission of which, I learned from a bit of research, was to "combat rural poverty" caused by the Depression. This involved persuading small farmers to sell their land and move with others to large farms (collectives or cooperatives) where they would work under the supervision of experts, presumably from D.C. This project failed because the farmers preferred living on their own land in poverty to being part of a collective farm. I was told that Bulow got him the job, and it must have been a good job. I doubt, though, that any of these towns was a desirable place to live in the late 1930s. In fact, given the depression and the drought, it is difficult to imagine any less desirable places to live in the whole country. There was most likely nothing to do in them on weekends but drink. Men would park their cars on Main Street on Saturday evening. Wives and kids would remain in the car and watch people walk by while father was in the pool hall with friends "hoisting a few."

By the time I began first grade in the fall of 1940 we were back in Rapid City. The only thing I remember about the school was that it had a huge covered slide for a fire escape. I'm told that I used to run home during recess, and Mom would have to take me back. (Apparently I didn't like the early grades, but the more I went to school, the more I like it, to such an extent, in fact, that I spent eleven years in institutions of higher learning!)

Another story that used to be told about me was that when I was getting vaccinations, I somehow got away from the doctor, ran out of the clinic and down the street with the syringe hanging from my arm. Sometime during the 1940-41 school year Mom decided she had had enough with Dad, his drinking, and inability to hold a job or support the family. More than one person urged her to divorce him, but Irish Catholic women of that era didn't get divorces. Even when I was in high school, "divorcee" was a dirty word. If she had divorced him, he would certainly have ended up "on the streets." Instead she decided to move the family back to the southeast corner of the state where our relatives lived. (An alternative might have been to put us kids, or some of us at least, up for adoption, something other families did during the Depression. More than once I heard Mom tell Dad that she had kept the family together in spite of him.) Cousin Gratten, the son of Mom's brother Paddy, drove out from their farm near Vermillion to Rapid City to pick us up. According to Joe she arranged all this by writing penny postcards. We didn't have a phone and, as a matter of fact, most of the people we might have called didn't have one either. I assume that our furniture and other possessions were stored in Rapid City, and the five of us squeezed into Paddy's car for the 400 mile trip. What luggage we had was strapped to the rear bumper. The only thing I remember about the trip was a comment by Gratten which was frequently repeated later. Someone, most likely Mom, said that there were only 100 miles or something like that left, and Grattan who hadn't been far away from home before, said, "Then I'd better get out and open the gate." I don't remember stopping to stretch our legs, get out to eat, or anything of that sort. (I don't recall, by the way, ever being hungry as a kid although Joe once said that he did. According to him, Mom used to stand at the kitchen door while we kids ate, and then she would eat the leftovers.)

When we arrived in Vermillion Mom, Carol, and I stayed with Mom's sister Vern Odeen and her husband Phil for a night or two. They lived on High Street in a house Tim O'Connor, Mom and Vern's father, had bought when he moved to town from the farm. The Odeens had one son at that time whom everyone called Kem. (Craig was born in 1943.) They had venetian blinds, a vacuum cleaner, and a camera, all things I had never seen before. They also had a telephone (88 was their number), and they showed us photos of the trip they had made to Mexico. They also had a new Ford. Uncle Phil owned a dairy called the Evergreen Farms and an ice cream store. We kids were sometimes allowed to finish off ice cream that was on the bottom of five gallon containers which was a big treat. The

Odeens were obviously much more affluent than we were, but then so was almost everyone else.

Mom rented a room in town for herself and Donna. Joe, Carol and I stayed with our Uncle Paddy and Aunt Margaret on the farm. I finished first grade at Greenfield country school. Joe and I used to walk to and from school about two miles each way. I don't remember much about school days there except that during recess the bigger boys played mumbling peg, a game played with a pocket knife. They like to frighten us little kids by threatening to castrate us with a knife as they did the pigs at home.

Summers on the farm were more pleasant. Pat and Margaret had a horse named Prince which we used to ride, and they had two dogs, a big one named Buck and a small one named Peggy. They also had a large kitchen table on which we played ping-pong after supper. Before going to bed the whole family would kneel in the living room and say the rosary, at least during Lent. Farmers in those days didn't have electricity or running water, and the toilet was a "two seater" out back behind the house. We all drank water from the same dipper which hung beside a crock full of water pumped up from underground by their windmill. Irons for ironing clothes were warmed up on the kitchen stove and held by removable wooden handles. Pat and Margaret did have one convenience which was a technological wonder for those days, a Maytag washing machine powered by a gas engine that had a long flexible exhaust pipe with a muffler on the end. It was stored on the porch most days, but on washing day it was moved out into the yard where someone would start it the way a person starts a motorcycle. Most people on farms washed clothes with a washboard as Mom did for us the following year. (In Ireland at the time some women did the laundry with their feet by stepping on the clothes in big tubs. In pictures they resemble Italians crushing grapes.)

Paddy used to entertain us kids with ghost stories; for instance he claimed a ghost had chased him around a haystack. He also did card tricks and other magic tricks. Whether his claim that he once stood on his head on the top of the windmill was true or not I never ascertained. He used to pay Carol and Kem to crawl under the granary and retrieve eggs which wayward hens had laid, something I couldn't do because I suffered from "hay fever." Unless my memory is deceiving me, Paddy ordered dentures from a catalogue. The company sent him an orange colored piece of wax which he bit into. The false teeth were then made to fit the impressions. It would be difficult to think of anyone more Irish than Paddy who even played the fiddle. All in all the days we spent on Pat and Margaret's farm were among the happiest of my childhood.

One day, as we were returning from town whither farm folks used to go on Saturday, we passed someone hitchhiking. Margaret said, "That looked like J.E." which is what folks around Beresford and Vermillion called Dad. They didn't stop, however. Sure enough later in the day Dad showed up at their farm. Conversations between Dad, Pat and Jack, Mom's other brother who lived on the next farm north, were usually about politics, especially Social Security, a favorite topic. Rather than being fruitful exchanges of opinions, these discussions were arguments used by Dad to show that he was a smarter than they were. It was the equivalent of rams butting heads. He had graduated from South Dakota State University and neither Paddy nor Jack had gone to high school. Ending education at eighth grade or even earlier was common for farm kids in the 1930s and '40s. I assume that Dad caught a ride later that day to Beresford where Gramma Reedy had a large house where he could stay. The following year I recall that he was at a CCC camp near Alcester, a town not far from Beresford.

Before the 1941-42 school year Mom got a job teaching in a country school called Newdale where she and Vern had taught before they were married. It was a two-room country school unlike most such schools which had only one room. Mom taught the older kids in grades seven and eight. Carol was in the first grade, and I was in second grade in the other room which was for grades one through six. I do not remember much about second grade except that I was constantly drawing pictures and hoped to become an artist or cartoonist. The other thing I remember about Newdale is that the students were split into two factions, those whose fathers had John Deere tractors and those who had Farmalls. Each faction thought its type of tractor was the best. (Before moving to Vermillion at the end of second grade, I worried that I might not have any friends there, and if so, I planned to start a controversy between kids whose families had Fords and those who had Chevys. In this way I reasoned I could at least have some of the class on my side. I was an *aficionado* of Chevies.)

During that year Mom rented a farmhouse and purchased a 1931 Chevy coupe which was needed to get to and from school as well as to and from town. Life in the rented farmhouse was Spartan, to engage in understatement. I doubt that we had much furniture. I remember a davenport that opened out and served as a bed. Carol slept with Mom in the bedroom except when Dad visited. There was an outdoor toilet, and we used kerosene lamps for light. We had a radio, but no refrigeration of any kind. (The following year when we moved to Vermillion, we had an ice box. The iceman would deliver a block of ice, the size, whether 25 pounds, 50 pounds, or 75 pounds, depended on which number was on the top of the card Mom would put in the window.)

I don't remember much regarding what we had to eat. I do know that Mom sometimes made cornmeal mush for breakfast. The origin of this as an Irish dish is explained by Cecil Woodham-Smith in *The Great Hunger*. When the potato crop failed, an attempt was made to replace potatoes with corn, some of which was sent by Native Americans to Ireland. Mom also used to make corn bread which was a favorite treat when served with butter and syrup. Most of the time we had margarine that was white and resembled lard. It had to be kneaded with a red pellet which turned it yellow so it looked more like butter. (I think the dairy farmers' lobby had something to do with this.) We kids didn't like it and wanted real butter not knowing anything about economics. One Christmas the Clarks who lived across the road invited us to Christmas dinner. Dad was home from the CCC camp, and he and Mom were looking forward to turkey or at least roast beef. Much to their disappointment we were served fish. Christmas had fallen on Friday that year, and the Clarks didn't know that Catholics could eat meat if a major holyday fell on Friday.

One of my chores that year was to take a gallon jug across the road to the Clarks and get it filled with milk. It would not have been a bad job except for the fact that the Clarks had dog I feared and hated. One evening I filled the jug with snow in our yard so I wouldn't have to deal with the hated dog. Mom was fooled until morning when the snow had melted and was reduced to water.

We didn't have a telephone, as I mentioned, but more affluent farmers did. At that time there would be several parties on the same line. Phones were on boxes on the wall, and each box had a little crank on the right side. Every home had its distinctive ring, a combination of longs and shorts. "Rubbering," as it was called, that is listening in on the neighbors' conversations, was a favorite pass time.

Winters were very severe, and I remember when Mom had to crank the car to get it started. Cranking was dangerous because the engine could kick and the crank could break a person's arm.

Dad was at the CCC camp, as was mentioned, and used to hitchhike home occasionally. I recall visiting him once at the camp. What struck me most were the huge bowls of fruit—big bright red apples and oranges and bananas which I don't think we had at home very often. When Dad came home, there were always arguments because he would want to take the car and drive to Beresford where he would borrow some money for whiskey from Gramma Reedy. Being poor is bad enough, but when you have one member of the family working against everyone else, it is unbearable.

The Clarks had two sons about my age so I had friends to play with. A favorite sport was to sit on the roof of the barn and throw sticks at their bull trying to make it mad. There were no little girls nearby for Carol to play with which is probably why she had two imaginary friends. When she and I played, we usually played "store" which involve taking what cans and jars there were in the pantry out and, I assume, pretend to buy and sell them. Mom entertained us by telling stories which she made up as she went. (Scholars have told me that these are the very best stories for kids.) For Christmas that year I received a piggy bank and a book entitled *365 Things to Do During the Coming Year*. I don't know how Mom managed to do it, but we also got a sled.

During the summer of 1942 Mom, Carol, and I lived with uncle Jack on his farm, and Mom helped take care of Jack's wife Anna Mary who was dying. Mom also taught us catechism in preparation for our First Communion. We were obliged to memorize answers to questions from the *Baltimore Catechism* and recite them when called upon by the priest. That summer may have been when I began my career as a cattle herder which I practiced for several summers. Jack would let the cattle graze in the ditches along the gravel road that passed his house, and it was my job to keep them from wondering too far away. It was a boring job, and I spent a lot of time throwing rocks at fence posts which may have helped prepare my arm for junior league baseball which I took up when we moved to town. On Saturdays we went to Vermillion, and Jack would sell cream at the dairy. He would then give me part of what he got for my salary. Unlike Uncle Pat, Jack never owned a tractor and farmed with horses until he retired and moved to Vermilion. He didn't have a windmill either, and another of my jobs was to keep the horse moving round and round which powered the pump that drew up water for the farm. On Saturdays we bathed, or at least I did, in a tub of hot water that was placed on the floor in the middle of the kitchen. (Oddly enough I can't remember anything about bathing at Paddy's farm. I can't remember about shampooing my hair either. Since farmers in those days didn't have showers, I'm not sure how we did it. I do recall that we males all used hair oil which later fell out of style and was ridiculed as "greasy kid stuff.") Jack did have one modern convenience a refrigerator which had a huge coil on top of it and was powered by natural gas.

Some time before the beginning of the '42-43 school year we moved to Vermillion, and Mom rented a house at 22 Washington Street. She began teaching at a country school west of Vermillion, and I attended third grade at Austin school which was just around the corner from where we lived. Carol would have been in second grade, and Joe in his junior year of high school. The house we lived in was a big square wooden box of a house. At the end of that year it was put up for sale for $1000, and we had to move since the family could not afford a down payment. I think Mom's salary was about $80 per month, and rent was about $30 per month. I remember that Mom bought me a blue suit from one of the neighbors, and I'm sure most of our clothes were second hand. My chief job on Washington Street was to carry tubs of cobs from the shed in the back of the house to a large box on the back porch. In the kitchen stove we burned cobs which we got for free from farmers. I don't think there was central heating in that house since there was a large stove in the living room which might have burned cobs too for all I know.

Joe had a job setting pins at the local bowling alley which contributed to the family's budget. Later he worked after school in a Gambles hardware store. In the absence of Dad, Joe was in effect the head of the family, and Mom relied on him tremendously. I believe Donna's first job was as a secretary in Sioux Falls. I got a paper route delivering "Grit," a weekly newspaper, but I never had more than half a dozen customers and made no money to speak of. (Anyone interested in "Grit" can read all about it on Wikipedia.) Every so often we would receive a postcard from Dad, but we didn't see much of him. He had found a job in a defense plant at Provo in the southwest corner of the state. When he did move back to Vermillion he sometimes drove a truck and delivered livestock to the stockyards in Sioux City. He also did construction work on several new buildings at the "U". Eventually he landed a job at the alfalfa plant on the "bottoms" of Vermillion where he worked for ten years. Dad was an extremely hard worker and was praised by several of his bosses.

Before the '45-46 school year we moved to 520 North Dakota St. where the family lived for nearly 20 years. The house was another big square white box but with a nice porch on both the main floor and the second story. With some landscaping and a paint job it could have been quite attractive. It was located across the street from the University of South Dakota which had lots of advantages for us kids including large fields for playing baseball and football. Also the "Armory" had an indoor pool where we were sometimes allowed to swim on Saturday mornings and a gymnasium where both Vermillion High School and the university basketball teams played their games. Living on Dakota Street meant that Carol and I went to Jolly School. I was in the fourth grade and also attended fifth and sixth grades there before going to junior and senior high school which were in the same building located near downtown. During the first three years of school I had attended four different schools so it was nice to be leading a more stable life. I don't remember much about Jolly School except the names of my teachers. Also it was in a better part of town, Austin School being on the "wrong side of the tracks," not literally but figuratively. Hence I became a friend of Jim Weeks whose father was president of the University. Sometimes after school I went home with Jim and played in the president's mansion which was by far the grandest house in town and certainly the most luxurious house I had ever seen. Brook Davis whose father owned a pharmacy was also a friend, and I sometimes went to his house after school too. Both Jim and Brook had chemistry sets, something I had never seen before. Brook also had a dark room in which he developed films. The three of us used to discuss inviting certain female classmates to Davis's house to pose nude so Brook could photograph them and develop the pictures. Needless to say, nothing ever came of those plans.

There is much more regarding our family life that is too painful to dwell on. Mom put up with Dad's (mis)behavior for at least twenty years. No one should have had to suffer as she did. A comment by the philosopher/theologian Michael Novak comes to mind. After a talk at Macalester, a student asked "What is God like?" Novak replied, "Jesus showed us what God is like; God is suffering love." We had in our own family an example of suffering love. I'm sure Mom has been rewarded with a high place in Heaven for what she suffered. All my life I have felt uncomfortable around men who for some reason reminded me of Dad.

In 1952 Dad suddenly stopped drinking, and never "fell off the wagon" from then until he passed away in 1976. Mom told me once she attributed Dad's sobriety to the prayers I was saying while at St. John's and St. Bonaventure's. Not long after 1952 he returned to the Church and the sacraments after a stay in the veterans' hospital. He attended Mass regularly for the rest of his life. After Mom passed away in 1965 he became an avid football fan, and he always enjoyed a good game of cards, especially "pitch" which was played for small amounts of money. He once told me that the twelve years from 1952 to 1964 when Mom was diagnosed with cancer were the happiest years of their lives. When I lived at home from 1960 to 1962, I used to come home in the evening and find them playing cards, and the love, happiness, and peace of mind were obvious. Mom's decision to "stick with it" paid off finally. He had put the family through hell for more than twenty years. What we didn't realize was that he was going through hell himself for all those years. Most likely the cause of his problems was hopelessness, the inability to see any end to the sufferings caused by the Great Depression. But in 1952 hope returned, and with the grace of God, he redeemed himself.

Joe with puppy, Uncle
Pat, Aunt Margaret,
Mom, Donna.
Little kids: "Kem"
(Phil) Odeen, the
author, Carol.

Mom and Dad *ca.* 1960

With new bike *ca.* 1946

520 N. Dakota St. where we lived in from 1943 to 1960.

Mom and Carol by our 1936 Ford.

Donna who passed away in 1978 at age 52.

Joe who served in the S.D. Legislature for fourteen years.

CHAPTER III

JUNIOR AND SENIOR HIGH SCHOOL

> Those who educate children
> well are more to be honored
> than parents, for these only gave
> life, those the art of living well.
> Aristotle

I have very little to say about junior high and high school. Junior hi was different from grade school because one took fewer subjects, had some choices, and went from classroom to classroom instead of spending the whole day in one room. Whereas in grade school it was common to like school and one's teachers, in the upper grades it was fasionable to dislike classes and to make fun of the faculty. The general atmosphere was very anti-intellectual, which is not surprising. Anyone who studied hard and got good grades was called a "brain," one of the dirtiest of words. I managed to get good grades without really trying. I will say, on the other hand, that the presence of the University of South Dakota in Vermillion probably made our schools more academically respectable than those in other towns in the state. Teachers could have continued their education by taking courses at USD, and I suppose some did. Also University faculty members with children the in Vermillion schools wanted them to get as good an education as possible, and hence watched carefully what was going on in their classes. Some teachers may well have been intimidated by the children of prominent University professors, and in our class we even had the son of the President of the University.

Among junior high teachers I remember Miss Blanchard and Mr. Van Gorcum with special affection. She taught us grammar including diagramming of sentences which unfortunately is rarely taught these days, and that stood me in good stead for later language studies. Mr Van Gorcum was a no-nonsense math teacher and basketball coach, and I learned a good deal from him. Mr. Rasmusson whom I had in high school was the first English teacher I encountered who could have been an actor; he brought literature to life for me. I'm glad I took biology and physics from Mr. Manley, but I'm sorry I never studied chemistry, a subject known for its "ubiquitous utility."

I loved "shop" and made some very nice pieces of furniture from wood. One semester we also drew blueprints which I really took to. (I remember telling my Dad that I was thinking of becoming an architect. His reply was, "You'll starve to death. There's a little building boom going on, but it will never last." That was the only conversation I ever had with him about a possible career. With few exceptions we kids, or at least I, rarely talked to Dad. Communication with him went through Mom. She would say, "Your Father thinks this or that." I assume she reported to him what we had said. Dad had no moral authority, and he knew it, and poor Mom was always in the middle.)

Band and athletics were as important, if not more important, than academic subjects. Thanks to Mr. Fejfar, I developed an appreciation for music although I discovered in college that I was no good on the baritone horn. Part of what made Fejfar an outstanding band director was his positive attitude and encouraging approach to everyone. I went out for basketball, football (one year only) and track. I did best at basketball (I hated football), and played it for two years in junior high and four years in high school. During my sophomore year I was one of the B team players who got to practice with the A team. One year the thought occurred to me that I had spent a lot of time on basketball, and I should either be good or quit. That motivated me to try harder, and I did get on the starting team for many games during my junior and senior years. Going to other towns for games was a "big deal" for us as were band trips.

I tried everything extracurricular. I was president of the class my sophomore year and on the student council the other three years. I sang in the glee club, was a cheer leader one year, in band all four years and in the all-state band my junior year. I was the business manager of the school paper a couple of years which meant I got out of classes to go downtown and sell ads. I belonged to the Latin club, went to Boys' State my junior year, and was student mayor of Vermillion for one day during my senior year. In spite of all of these activities I think I devoted most of my energy to getting a "rise" out of my buddies or at least a laugh.

For entertainment, besides athletic games, there were movies which cost a dime. Vermillion had two theaters, the Co-ed and the March Theater both owned by the same man. The March showed only westerns. Favorite actors were Abbot and Costello, Van Johnson, Jimmy Stewart, Rita Hayworth, Doris Day, and Judy Garland. Before the main feature there were newsreels which kept us up to date on world events. This was especially important before the advent of TV. At the Co-ed every other row had a "love seat" on the left end. I once sat with a girl I liked and watched the move "The Thing."

Family entertainment was limited to Sunday dinners with relatives. For years Uncle Jack would come over on Sunday, always bringing a half-gallon of ice cream. Jack lived alone and often listened to ball games on the radio at night in the dark presumably to save electricity. It was fashionable to make fun of TV, but I think it enriched the folks' lives immensely. Mom liked Tennessee Ernie Ford and Mitch Miller. Dad became an avid fan of football.

My friends and I were all passionately interested in cars. This was partly due to the fact that during World War II no new cars were manufactured. G.M., Ford, Chrysler, and other manufacturers were making vehicles for the armed services. When new models of cars appeared in 1946 there was great excitement. Besides the "big three" there were Hudsons, Studebakers, and Nashes, and Chrysler made DeSotos until 1961. When I was in junior hi, a friend and I used to sit in a tree on the boulevard with clipboards in hand and record the year, make and model of each car that passed by.

My first job was at Sletwold's Flower Shop. It involved delivering for the most part, and I was paid 25 cents per hour. What irked me was that a few minutes before quitting time they would load me down with bouquets and ask me to drop them off on my way home. The only problem was that some were for the hospital which was at one end of the town and others for the university which was at the other end. When I learned that the girls who worked in the corner ice cream store were making 75 cents per hour, I applied there and got hired. I worked for Austin Dairy for a total of eight years, mostly at the Ice Cream Store, but for several summers I worked at the dairy where I helped make ice cream, butter, cottage cheese, popsicles, etc. and also picked up milk from farmers and delivered milk in town. I could well have made a career of it.

I graduated from high school with no plans for the following fall even though I was an honor student. I never talked to my parents about going to college, and schools in those days didn't have "guidance counselors."

The fact that we lived across the street from the university made this even stranger. In a way I think that my parents never recovered from the depression. The depression, I assume, was such a horrible experience that it destroyed my parents' ability to dream, even for their kids. They certainly didn't push any of us the way immigrant parents do—pushing them into law or medicine or some lucrative field. Immigrants come to this country with the idea that it is the "land of opportunity" which it is, but that had not been my parents' experience.

"A" Basketball

Vermillion High basketball team, 1952.

At State Game Lodge with Tom Michaels
and Model A Ford we bought for $50.00.

CHAPTER IV

IN, OUT AND BACK IN THE SEMINARY

Many are called but few are chosen.
Matthew 22:14

It must have been some time during my sophomore year of high school that Father Wolf, our pastor, began kidding me and my friend Pat Merrigan about trying the seminary. Most likely during my junior year of high school I decided to do so because I registered for elementary Latin in my senior year. Of course, I said nothing to anyone, nor did I change my "lifestyle" at all; for example, I continued dating girls. In fact, I even found a girlfriend in elementary Latin which I was taking with the seminary in mind!

Fr. Wolf was a good priest, but naturally he had his faults. Some members of the parish didn't like the fact that he entertained the "upper crust" (both Catholics and Protestants) with cocktail parties. Also his housekeeper was unpopular with members of the parish because she was reputed to be an outstanding cook and hostess. No one could criticize Fr. Wolf, however, for lacking zeal. He was the *defensor fidei* par excellence. If a USD student mentioned to Fr. Wolf that a professor had made anti-Catholic remarks in class or even insinuated something negative about the Church, Fr. Wolf would be in his office next morning to set him straight. Unfortunately zeal can affect one's judgment adversely, and urging me to try the seminary probably showed bad judgment on Fr. Wolf's part.

After graduating from high school in the spring of 1952, I spent the summer working at the State Game Lodge in the Black Hills as a bell boy. It was a wonderful job. A favorite part of my job was to ride a motor scooter and lead people who had rented cabins to the proper one. There were also lots of things to do when we weren't working: we went horseback riding and hiking, and there were square dances and parties. Quite often we went into Custer, and few times we went to Rapid City. We were also allowed to take the Lodge's station wagon and go to Spearfish to see the Passion Play. I can't remember exactly how it happened, but the Fr. Wolf must have contacted me while I was at the Game Lodge and told me that if I wanted to go to St. John's, the bishop would pay my tuition and other expenses. Again he stressed that, of course, I had nothing to lose. Hence I decided to try it out, and the following September the folks drove me up to Collegeville.

I was very fond of St. John's and of the Benedictines, and in fact I still am. As I write this I am in the process of becoming an Oblate of St. Benedict. In the 1950s St. John's was the world's largest Benedictine monastery. Many of monks had doctorates and had studied in Europe at Louvain or Innsbruck or Rome. I was impressed by their erudition and inspired by their dedication and holiness.

There were about eighty of us in the first-year class. We lived in what was called St. Anselm's Hall (affectionately known as "Slime Hall"). Each person had a desk in the study hall and a locker upstairs outside the dormitory. The dormitory was a very large room with perhaps eighty beds in it. Beside each bed there was a stool, and that was it for furnishings. In the morning we dressed in front of our locker, then we took our mirror and shaving kit and stood in line to get to a sink. There was no privacy, and nobody was ever alone. In the winter it was extremely cold. Collegeville is eighty miles north of the Twin Cities, and in those days it was not uncommon to have temperatures of 25 or 30 below zero in mid winter. It is hard to imagine a more spartan life, but I took to it and loved it.

I recall studying Latin which I liked, and I took first-year Greek with Fr. Cosmos. Besides that I know I had the History of Western Civilization taught by Fr. Vincent, Religion with Father Lancelot, and Freshman English with Fr. Conrad. I don't think I took science, and I can't remember what the other subjects were. I do remember, being inspired by the Benedictines and disciplining myself to study for two or three hours without getting up even for a drink of water. My parents spent sent me $15 a month for an allowance which sufficed since we were allowed to go to town, that is to St. Cloud, only once a month. Even though I liked St. John's very much, for some reason during the summer of 1953 I decided not to go back. Obviously I didn't know what I was doing or wanted to do.

My sophomore year of college was spent at the University of South Dakota. Again I took Latin and Greek, both from Grace Beede about whom I will have much to say later. I recall an English course, a speech course, and I took Spanish from Dr. Arnaud. Other than these I can't remember what I took, but I do remember being very unhappy. I'm not exactly sure why, but it is the case that Father Wolf had been critical of the university, comparing it unfavorably with Jesuit schools in the east and denouncing it as a hot bed of atheism and anti-Catholic sentiments. Probably too I was unhappy with the social life since I didn't like the drinking and carousing that went on in fraternities, but students who were independents were on the outside looking in as far as a social life was concerned. I also lacked the intellectual stimulation and companionship I had enjoyed at St. John's. It could be true that living at home wasn't all that good. In any case sometime during that that year I decided that I would go back to the seminary. Fr. Wolf, who was originally from Buffalo, New York and had attended St. Bonaventure, suggested that I go there. (To digress for a moment I recall one year—probably 1967 or 1968—when I was a high school teacher of Latin and a guidance counselor for a semester at a girls school in Adrian, Michigan. The principal told me that I could tell which girls were unhappy at home because they would talk about going far away. Sure enough, girls would come in and tell me they wanted to join the Peace Corps and go to Africa or they wanted to go to South America or some place far from home. The principal was right, and this may have been a true of me too.) In any case I had a desire to get far away certainly not from my Mother but most likely from my Dad. So when Father Wolf suggested trying St. Bonaventure's which was outside Olean, New York, I like the idea very much. Fr. Wolf obviously had a good deal of influence with the bishop since again, one phone call, and the bishop agreed to cover tuition, books, etc.

St. Bonaventure's was run by the Franciscans who turned out to be quite different from the Benedictines. While there were some famous scholars at St. Bonaventure's such as the Rector of the Seminary, Fr. Thomas Plassman, a scripture scholar, Alan Wolter, an expert on Duns Scotus, and Philotheus Boehner, an expert on William of Ockham, there were also some who were teaching subjects they knew little about. One year the church historian was obliged to teach American history because it was a required course. He sat in front of the class with the textbook in front of him and turned page after page telling us what was on each page. The Franciscan order seemed to attract non-conformists; every friar was an individual. The Benedictine way of life attracted me, but I never thought about joining the Franciscans. The best thing about St. Bonaventure was the friends I made there, especially David Hyman who joined the Franciscans and with whom I am still in touch.

CHAPTER V

WHEN IN ROME . . .

O Roma felix,
quae duorum Principum
es consecrata glorioso sanguine!
Author unknown

During Christmas vacation in 1955 I was home from St. Bonaventure's, and I recall meeting with Fr. Wolf in his office. I can't remember if it was his idea or mine, but Rome and the possibility of studying there came up. I had done well at St. Bonaventure's and before that at St. John's, getting mostly A's. Much to my surprise Fr. Wolf picked up the telephone and called Bishop Brady in Sioux Falls using a special, private number. They chatted briefly regarding my studying in Rome and that was it. The bishop would send me in the fall of 1956 to the North American College (NAC hereafter). I'm not sure if I told my folks then or later; most likely I couldn't keep the news to myself.

Back in Bonaventure's after vacation it caused quite a sensation. Every spring a couple of students from Buffalo would be informed that they were being sent to Rome in the fall, but this was January and I was teased for a whole semester about being an "apprentice to the Pope", eventually becoming a bishop, etc.

During the summer of 1956 I learned somehow that a friend from St. John's, Gerry Sande, a native of North Dakota, was headed for Rome also. We met in New York City and sailed on the Maasdam to Southampton, England. Before setting off for New York the family had a "Last Supper" at the farm of my sister Donna and her husband Bud. I was leaving for four years so it was very sad, especially for Mom whom I had only seen cry once or twice before. Only years later when I had my own kids did I realize what she was experiencing and would experience. The following morning

Donna and Bud drove me to Minneapolis where I stayed with a friend from Vermillion High School, Jack Donahoe, who showed me around the Twin Cities. Next day I left by train for New York City where cousin Eileen, aunt Mamie from D.C., and Jim Lafferty, a friend from St. Bonaventure's, saw me off on the ship. (Everybody in those days crossed the Atlantic by ship; jets were just becoming available. A couple of years later, when students at the North American College began chartering jet planes to bring their families to Rome for ordination, it was an exciting innovation.)

In London Sande and I stayed with Mrs. Lynch who ran a pension which was a favorite with students from the North American College. (Sande had received a list of pensions and small hotels from a friend at the North American College.) Mrs. Lynch and her husband entertained us by taking us to the local pub where we met their neighbors who teased us about celibacy, wearing hair shirts, etc. We spent a few days sightseeing in London. From London we went to Paris where we stayed in a place that was also popular with the students from the NAC, the Hotel d'Athens. We visited the usual sites in Paris, and then we flew to Rome. I remember how thrilled I was to see St. Peter's, the Forum, the Colosseum and other famous Roman sites from the air.

I loved everything about Rome and Italy—the food, the music, the people, the scenery, the antiquities, the churches, etc. It was the first time I'd been in a foreign country except for the few days in London and Paris. First of all, I loved Italian, and I was determined to master it to the extent possible. I envied European students who were often fluent in three or four languages. There were some American students, on the other hand, who had spent four years in Rome and knew only a few phrases of Italian. I carried my dictionary with me at all times, constantly looking up words. I walked around town reading signs. Sometimes I stopped people and asked questions, for instance for directions, just to see if they understood me and if I could understand them. (I was surprised to learn that some people, but only a few, wouldn't talk to a person who was wearing a cassock! Anticlericalism was a totally new thing to me. No one ever spat on me, but there were parts of town, e.g. Trastevere, where people, most likely communists, would spit on the sidewalk in front of clerics.) At night before falling asleep I carried on the imaginary conversations with myself in Italian. I was always asking how would one say this or that in Italian. Once classes started I practiced Italian with a student from Spain who was much better at it than I was, Spanish being much closer to Italian than English is. Between other classes he and I practiced English for his benefit.

The second year I did the same thing with a French student who helped me with French in return for my helping him with English.

I also loved Latin and paid close attention to lectures at the Gregorian University although I must admit that before Vatican II, Catholic theology was very boring. (More about this later.) The Gregorian was and is the Oxford of theological schools. Founded in 1551, it was run by the Jesuits. The "Greg" was the essence of simplicity, consisting of one building in the middle of town about one block from the Trevi Fountain. There was no campus, just a busy piazza in front. Classes met in a large aula that held perhaps 300 students. Instruction was completely by a lecture. There were no discussions, no term papers, and no one ever interrupted the professor with a question, nor was anyone ever called upon. Each morning we went by school bus from the NAC to the Greg where we had four hours of classes separated by breaks of ten minutes. Everything was in Latin—the lectures, the books, and the exams, both oral and written. Most courses lasted the whole school year, and most exams were oral coming in the spring after what we called the "big push," the couple of months of preparation. The grade for the whole year depended upon one oral exam that might last less than a half hour. For most courses we were given a sheet of theses which we were supposed to be prepared to defend at the final exam. It was the medieval scholastic approach, pure and simple. For most of us it was a matter of memorization—the process wasn't much different from what we had gone through as kids in catechism. Americans generally were weaker in Latin than their fellow students from Europe. For instance, the Germans, many of whom had attended Classical Gymnasia where they studied Latin for maybe eight years and Greek for perhaps five years before arriving in Rome. Americans typically didn't understand the lectures at the Greg during the first year until after Christmas. (Classes began in October.)

The faculty, of course, consisted of top scholars from all over the world. Among the most famous was Bernard Lonergan, a Canadian, whose book *Insight, A Study of Human Understanding* came out that fall. I remember his course which was called *De Verbo Incarnato*. Other luminaries included Joseph Fuchs, a charismatic lecturer who taught moral theology and later became internationally famous. Fr. Trump taught *De Ecclesia* ("on the Church") and was rumored to have written an encyclical letter (or at least the first draft) for Pius XII. I also had "Pappy" Hurth who must have been eighty and was said to be the Pope's confessor. (Yes, the Pope goes to confession.) Back at the NAC during the first year we had reviews in

English in the evening taught by Fr. Willie which were designed to help us until our Latin was up to speed.

The North American College is located on the Janiculum hill just south of Vatican City. The building itself was very new having been being after World War II and consisted of a quadrangle with one wing added on the south. From the air the it would have resembled a squared off letter P. Within the quadrangle there was a "cortile" (court yard) with a pool and forty-eight orange trees, one for each state. Outside along the south wing there were handball courts, tennis courts, and a field for softball and touch football. Each student had a private room with a desk, a bed and a small area rug plus a bookcase. Visiting others' rooms was not permitted. The floors were marble as were the door frames; marble, I was told, being cheaper in Italy than wood. Visitors might consider the building quite luxurious, and it was in many ways. A joke was that, if a civil war broke out between the Communists and other political parties, we wouldn't have to worry about an attack since both sides would want our building for their headquarters after the war. Living there was, however, not always easy. For one thing it was easy to be lonely, and in the winter it was very chilly since there was no central heating. Many students studied with an overcoat on plus an extra pair of socks and sometimes even gloves. There was hot water only at certain times of the day, fuel oil being very expensive in Italy even then.

Daily life was highly regimented, as one would expect, but this did not bother me since I like a scheduled life. We rose early (5:00 or 5:30) and were to be in the chapel for morning prayers at 6:00, followed by Mass. After Mass there was breakfast and one half hour or so to make one's bed and straighten up one's room. Then school buses arrived to take us to the Gregorian University for four hours of classes. The buses returned us to the NAC at noon for lunch which was followed by an hour for a siesta. Recreation was required in the afternoon, and no one was supposed to be in his room during that time.

The main type of recreation was taking walks with one's "camerata." A camerata was a group of from 7-10 students headed by a prefect, typically a third-year student, and a beadle, usually a second-year student. Monday, Wednesday and Friday, we set out on foot for a specific destination usually a church (Rome was said to have 600 churches) or an historical site such as the Roman Forum or the Circus Maximus. While on these walks we were not allowed to enter cafes or bars or even stores. Shopping or having coffee or a beer or glass of wine was only allowed on weekends when one got permission and wore a plain black cassock not the usual cassock of

NAC which had a dark red sash and blue piping. Obviously it would have caused scandal if a large number of American students in their distinctive garb gathered in a bar or a *trattoria* and spent the afternoon drinking wine and eating. Thanks to these walks we got to know the city, its history, topography, culture, and architecture very well. On other days one could engage in sports or read or talk with friends in the recreation room.

A favorite indoor sport in those days was "crashing the gate" at ceremonies at St. Peter's. In the 1950s there was little or no security. Italians used to drive into St. Peter's Square when there was a breeze and wash their Fiats by the water fountains. Moreover anyone wearing a cassock was considered a priest so it was very easy to walk quickly past the Swiss guards into St. Peter's Basilica. For special events one needed a ticket (a *bigletto* in Italian), a large piece of paper about 4" x 6". There were different colored tickets for different parts of the Basilica on different days. Most of us had a file of old tickets. On the day of a special event such as a canonization, Papal Mass or other ceremony, we would stand a ways away from the entrance to the church and observe what color of ticket was being used for the best seats that day. We would then fish out from our file a ticket of the right color, walk quickly past the guards flashing it, and take our seat up front.

A couple of examples: at one of Pope Pius XII's nine funeral masses, I stood by a side entrance to St. Peter's until I discovered which tickets were getting people the best seats that day. Then I walked by the guards and straight into a section to the side of the main altar. At first I was the only person sitting there, but gradually others arrived—ambassadors wearing tuxes, ribbons, medals etc. moved in around me. I was sitting in a section reserved for the *corpo diplomatico!* Eventually John Foster Dulles, who was representing Eisenhower, and other distinguished guests arrived and sat in the row right ahead of me.

I also had a front row seat for the entombment of Pius XII. That was the ceremony during which his body was placed in a coffin which was then placed inside another coffin and then slowly lowered into the crypt below St. Peter's. I was standing beside Archbishop Cody (later Cardinal Cody) who was joking about the "papal *plumbatori*" who used rubber hammers to pound the cover onto the Pope's coffin.

For the coronation of Pope John XXIII a friend and I were standing at the foot of the Scala Regia, the stairway to the right of St. Peter's which leads up into the Vatican Palace. Cardinals and bishops were arriving with chaplains whose job it was to hold their vestments as they ascended and descended the stairs. After observing what was going on, we eventually joined the procession. The Cardinals and bishops who didn't have their own chaplains presumably thought we had been assigned to accompany them. We ended up in a large room upstairs in the Vatican Palace where the members of the hierarchy were lining up for the procession to St. Peter's. Bishop Fulton Sheen was there, but Cardinal Siri from Genoa who was being sued by the Communist Party was the center of attention. We proceeded into the Basilica beside the prelates and walked straight up to the main altar. Classmates and friends who were in the back of the church, about one-eighth of a mile from the front, were amazed to see us in the procession. From that point I recall moving around from place to place, and at one time I even had a better seat than the Pope! In those days an assassin could easily have disguised himself as a priest and got very close to his target.

When Pius XII died, we had just returned from the Villa where we spent our summers to the NAC for a retreat, a week long silent retreat in preparation for the beginning of the school year. One morning when we arrived at chapel there was black bunting on the entrance, and we knew exactly what had happened since it had been rumored from some time that the Pope was not well. Soon the rector, Bishop O'Connor, arrived and announced that the Holy Father had indeed passed away during the night. Since the American College was one of his favorite colleges, we were told that students from our college would be going to Castelgondolfo, the Pope's summer residence where he had died, to serve as an honor guard at the bedside of the deceased pontiff. Later in the morning a list was posted on the bulletin board giving the names of students who were going to form the honor guard. Names were listed "according to seniority" (which was the way everything was done), and lucky me, my name was the very last one on the list. Later that afternoon a group of us took a taxi and headed for Castelgondolfo. One member of the group was Larry Seubert, one of my best friends whom I later met up with in Ann Arbor and then in the Twin Cities. It turned out that there was a traffic jam about twenty-five miles long from the outskirts of Rome to the Pope's summer residence. We were one of the few groups who got through the traffic, and we ended up at the papal residence where we were led upstairs into a room adjoining the bedroom where the Holy Father's body was lying on his bed. Every so often a group of us would be a led in to kneel at the side of the bed or rather around the bed. Much to our surprise the body of Pius XII was wrapped in what appeared to be Glad Wrap or plastic wrap of some sort. We would knee by the bed for a time and then return to the adjoining room where we rested and perhaps prayed and talked to one another. Because of the traffic jam very few fellow students from the NAC ever arrived. Most likely again because of the traffic jam we couldn't get back to Rome so we spent most of the night there. I recall returning to Rome very early in the morning and asking the taxi driver to stop so that we could pick up newspapers knowing that this was a historic moment. Pius XII had been Pope since 1939 and had reigned for as long as any of us could remember.

Another feature of life at NAC was showing visitors around the building. Each day a student would be excused from attending classes to serve as a guide. I recall showing Jefferson Caffrey and his wife around. He had been U.S. ambassador to various countries including, I believe, Spain and France. I was called to the Rector's office where he introduced me to the Caffreys—all in Italian for some reason. Fortunately my Italian was up to par, and when the Rector asked me to give them a tour, I replied "*con piacere, Excellenza*" (with pleasure, Your Excellence.) Bishop O'Connor who must have weighed 300 pounds, had a "penchant for pomposity," as George Schlichte wrote in his book *Politics in the Purple Kingdom*; he never forgot for a moment that he was a bishop. On another occasion I was showing an army chaplain the college. He was a crusty old fellow who had seen plenty of the seamy side of life during World War II. Just before the tour he had met the Rector, and he was still shaking his head and saying that there was more pomp and circumstance associated with meeting Bishop O'Connor than at a Papal audience. After the Bishop celebrated High Mass for us, there would be a servant wearing white gloves, holding a silver tray with a glass of Fuggi water waiting in the sacristy for him. (For an unflattering portrait of Bishop O'Connor [no relation of ours] see Schlichte's book. Msgr Schlichte was the *Economo* or Business Manager at NAC during my day. After years in Rome consorting with high Church officials including attending the conclave that elected John XXIII as one of Cardinal Spellman's chaplains, he served as head of a seminary in Boston before being laicized and marrying late in life.)

Whether at St. John's, St. Bonaventure's or NAC I was one of what some wags called "the Brethren of the Strict Observance," i.e. I never broke a rule; in fact I never even thought of breaking a rule. There were some guys who did break rules, for instance skipping classes to drink coffee and chat with friends, or perhaps skip classes to catch up on sleep. I can honestly say I never did. I was the typical pre-Vatican II Catholic who had been brought up on "Holy Obedience." We were taught to see the rules of the institution and the will of superiors as the will of God, and it was by obeying these that we were to sanctify ourselves. To go even further, we should take Meister Ekhard's advice and strive to become "will-less," that is give up our own will completely and let God's will replace it. Then we could say with St. Paul, "I live no longer I, but Christ liveth in me." (Galatians 2:20) The one or two rebels who were in our class didn't speak out against current practices; they just broke rules until they got caught and were advised to leave or were expelled. An academic system that stresses memorization of subject matter à la catechism and a regime based on obedience does not produce critical thinkers who are going to "think outside the box." Nevertheless, I had no complaints.

Had I stayed another month, I might have stayed for ordination because the election of John XXIII changed everything. Whereas Pius XII was a member of the nobility and appeared to be aloof, cold and rigid, John XXIII came from a peasant family, was a roly poly, jolly fellow who was said to love good food, good wine, and an occasional cigar. Suddenly Christianity became a religion of joy and love rather than one with emphasis on asceticism and obedience to rules. Never was it more clear that the man at the top (and in the case of the Church I don't have to say "or woman") makes a huge difference. What Pope John and Vatican II achieved, to put it simply, was to turn the pyramid upside down. For centuries the Church was thought of as the hierarchy—priests, bishops, archbishops, cardinals, and the Pope. Now the Church became the "People of God" and the clergy became their servants. It was a change of epic proportions.

Although, as I said, there were few rebels or reformers at NAC in my day, there were three things that bothered me and still bother me.

First of all, I think it is a mistake to require all priests to take a vow of celibacy. I think the Catholic Church should do what the Orthodox Churches do, i.e. require those who want to be monks to be celibate but allow parish priests to marry. This would solve many problems, for example, the shortage of priests. Certainly some day this will be the practice. The pressure the vow of celibacy put on seminarians was something terrible. I remember the case of a student a year ahead of me. He had been made a subdeacon and then a deacon, and his family and other relatives had come to Rome for his ordination to the priesthood. The night before the ceremony, he changed his mind causing untold grief to his parents and others. There was another young man who got ordained, when home, and a short time later lost his faith, left the priesthood, and married causing a huge scandal.

Secondly I think it is unreasonable to require a young man of twenty-four to take vows that will bind him for the rest of his life. It could just as well be for a period of three years or perhaps five years. Of course the situation today is totally different. In the late fifties and early sixties no one ever mentioned "laicization." We were too pious to even think of it. Ordination to the priesthood was forever and left an "indelible mark" on an individual's soul. It is not easy to find reliable statistics, but according to David Rice, author of *Shattered Vows: Exodus from the Priesthood* approximately 100,000 priests worldwide left the priesthood "during the past twenty-five years" and that was in 1989! In 1950 in the U.S. there were 652 Catholics per priest, most of whom were in active ministry. By 2000, there were 1,257 Catholics per priest, and nearly a third of all priests are retired or over the age of 70. The number of seminarians has also plummeted, and ordinations are not keeping up with deaths. Christianity has "crashed" in Europe, as one author put it, but the Church is growing and flourishing in Africa and Asia. (As I write this I am teaching "Ecclesiastical Latin" to seminarians at the School of Divinity of the University of St. Thomas. A student who is taking a course called "Holy Orders" showed me a two-page form which was distributed in class. It is a "Rescript from the Congregation for the Clergy" in Rome telling priests how to submit a petition to be dispensed from "all the obligations connected to sacred Ordination." All that is required is the bishop's signature. My, how times have changed!)

Thirdly there is *parvitas materiae,* i.e. parvity or "smallness" of matter. Let me illustrate my interpretation of this using the following example. If one steals a dime, it is less sinful than if one steals $1000, and to steal $20,000 is a more serious sin than stealing $1,000. In other words, the less "matter" there is, the less sinful the act is. In "sins of unchastity," however, there is no smallness of matter; hence as far as lust is concerned, all sins are mortal sins provided there is full consent. To give full consent to venereal pleasure for even a few seconds is as sinful as committing adultery. Although I have found very little literature on this subject, I can think of two reasons for this teaching: in the first place there is a commandment that says "Thou shalt not covet thy neighbor's wife," and to violate a commandment must always be serious. Secondly, in matters of lust where would one draw the line between venial sins and mortal sins? What made the whole issue even more worrisome was that in the case of a priest bound by a vow of chastity, any violation would be not only a mortal sin but a sacrilege. Charles Curran, who was one year ahead of me at the NAC and who has written an autobiography entitled *Loyal Dissent,* claims that he was the first American theologian to challenge the traditional teaching. Curran is one of the best known theologians in the U.S. He is the author of numerous books and hundreds of articles. He is not allowed, however, by the Vatican to call himself a Catholic theologian and has been teaching for many years at Southern Methodist University.

I was thinking seriously about leaving and casually confided my uncertainty to a priest on the staff as I asked for special permission to go shopping. Much to my surprise when I return from town there was a note on my door telling me to go to the Rector's office. The rector was Bishop O'Connor. He informed me that Monsignor Marshall had reported that I was leaving. He then proceeded to tell me how to ship my books, etc., where to get a ticket and told me to keep my plans secret lest I upset friends and classmates. Things moved ahead more quickly than I had expected.

Before the ship was to sail, I did manage to spend a few days in Florence with my high school friend, Pat Merrigan, who was on leave from service in the army in Germany. From Florence I took the train to Naples where I was to catch the Italian liner Saturnia. From the train station I took a taxi to the dock. The driver drove around from pier to pier searching for the ship. Finally he asked someone, *"Dov' e la Saturnia?"* (Where is the Saturnia?) To which the reply was *"E gia partita!"*—(It already left). As I was trying to recover from this shock, an Italian-American showed up in another taxi also looking for the Saturnia. Before long a small crowd gathered. Some of us took a taxi to the headquarters of the shipline where we were told that the crew of our ship had threatened to go on strike, but if the ship didn't enter the harbor, their contract prevented them from doing so. Hence the ship had remained on the high seas, and the company had notified all the passengers whose addresses they had, but unfortunately they had been unable to contact us. Those who had received notice and had come early and were taken by tender to the Saturnia which was now half way to Barcelona! On the verge of desperation, I was wondering if I could return to NAC until the next ship arrived. Much to our surprise we were then told that the company would put us up in a hotel and the next morning pay our way by plane to Barcelona where we could catch the ship, and that is what happened. Another close call! Naples is not a place to be stranded.

Thanks to the fact that I played bridge, I became acquainted with most of the bridge players in second class. Among them was a young lady from Germany who was also friendly with some crew members. The crew were sponsoring a beauty contest. They would invite the best looking female passengers to the officers' quarters to be photographed in their swimming suits. The photos were then posted on the wall, and before the end of the voyage the crew would select "Miss Saturnia." Only the most naïve would fail to recognize their real intentions. In any case through this German girl I got invited to a party in the officers' quarters where there was a good deal of drinking, laughing and celebrating. Believe it or not, some of us were invited to go up on the bridge and take turns steering the ship! This was two years after the Italian liner the Andrea Doria, the pride of Italy, sank after colliding with the Stockholm. I wonder who was steering it at the time.

Two years at NAC had a profound and lasting influence on my life. It gave me a love of the Church, of Latin and of Italian that is with me to this day. It also stimulated my interest in philosophy, theology, history, Italian literature, archeology, architecture, art and opera. No doubt my fondness of the early morning and practice of rising at 5:00 a.m., my taking a siesta, and leading a scheduled life in an attempt to avoid wasting time derive from those days in Rome. Even the practice of diverting myself during the dead of winter by planning a summer trip has stayed with me. Four years after retiring I have resumed the practice of meditating and doing spiritual reading.

North American College, Rome, 1958.

CHAPTER VI

SUMMER TRIPS

> Not all who wander are lost.
> J.F.R. Tolkien

Another feature of life in Rome was the summer trip. Each of us could travel for a month during summer vacation, but if a member of one's family came over, we could travel longer, six weeks or even two months. There were also some established itineraries. One was the "shrine run" and another was the "beer run." My first summer, the summer of 1957 I traveled with Victor Galeone and Ralph Platz on the "shrine run." We flew to Barcelona on a cheap student flight, did some sight seeing there which included a one-day pilgrimage to the Benedictine monastery at Monserrat which is associated with St. Ignatius of Loyola, the founder of the Society of Jesus (the Jesuits). From Barcelona we flew to Madrid near which there were a number of places of interest to us, e.g. Toledo, El Escorial, burial place of Spanish kings, and Avila where the shrine of St. Teresa of Avila, Carmelite nun and mystic, is located.

From Madrid we had planned to take the train to Granada, but after wasting most of a day in the train station trying unsuccessfully to get tickets, we gave up and took the train to Malaga. (We stood in a long line to get tickets only to be told once we got to the window that tickets to Granada wouldn't go on sale until noon. After standing in another long line at noon, the window was closed just as it was our turn to buy tickets, etc.) Malaga had a beautiful beach which we had to ourselves although I've heard that today it is like Miami Beach. Still wanting to see the Alhambra and other sights in Granada associated with the Muslim kings who ruled that part of Spain, we hired a car and a driver for a very reasonable price to drive us there in the morning and return us to Malaga in the evening. (I can't recall where we (I especially) got the money for a trip such as this. Perhaps I managed to save it from my $25 a month allowance my folks sent me. It is true, however, that in those days the dollar was very strong, and we stayed in very inexpensive places and often bought food from street vendors.)

From Madrid we took a train to Lisbon where we did sight seeing (visiting mainly churches and monasteries), but our real reason for going to Portugal was to visit the shrine at Fatima. After a long trip back to Madrid we went to San Sabastian in the Basque country where we had a friend from the Greg. He showed us the town which was beautiful. (Franco spent his summers there, and his yacht was in the harbor.) Our friend told us that one of the vices of the Basques was gluttony, and the bishop had had to put limits on post-ordination banquets lest they scandalize the laity. Next came Lourdes which I found much more moving than Fatima. Especially inspiring at Lourdes was the nighttime candle procession with everyone singing familiar hymns. Next stop was the home of St. Jean Vianney, known as the Cure d'Ars, whose below average IQ made Latin, philosophy and theology too difficult for him, but the bishop ordained him anyway, and he because famous through France as a confessor and saint.

The next to the last stop was Paray-le-Monial, the home of St. Margaret Mary Alacoque famous for promoting devotion to the Sacred Heart. (We were on the French Riviera, but we spent almost all of our time in shrines and churches! Of course, we attended Mass everyday during summer trips.) Back in Italy we spent a couple of days with Victor Galeone's relatives in Viareggio, on the coast of Italy. They were people of ordinary means, but la Mama put on unbelievably sumptuous feasts for us—tons of hors d'oeuvres, pasta and desserts. If one didn't literally stuff himself she would say, "*Non ti piace?*"—Don't you like it? Isn't it good enough for you? (Italian women show their love by the food they cook.) They had three daughters who, we were told, were upset because we used the formal "*lei*" instead of the familiar "*tu*" when we spoke to them. My problem was not stuffiness—I had never learned the familiar verb forms! Finally we arrived back in Rome or rather to the summer villa near Castelgondolfo exhausted, relaxed, and no doubt nearly penniless.

As mentioned above, if a family member came to Italy to travel, we were allowed to be gone for more than a month. Hence the second summer (1958) my sister Carol came to Rome, and we set out on what now looks like an epic journey from Italy to North Ireland and Scotland. I will give our itinerary, leaving out detailed descriptions. After showing Carol the sights of Rome (St. Peter's, catacombs, Forum, Circus Maximus, etc.) our first stop was Viareggio where one of Victor Galeone's cousins showed us the town. We traveled through Switzerland, visited Munich (and the Hofbrau House), took a boat ride on the Rhine from Koblenz to Cologne whence we made out way to Brussels for the World's Fair (Expo '58), our first major goal. At the World's Fair we stayed in youth hostels, which as I recall, were tents with cots in them. Elsewhere we stayed in inexpensive *"pensioni"* although again I am not sure how I, at least, financed this trip. Carol had been teaching and earning a good salary. From Brussels we stopped in Paris for a few days, and then went to London before arriving at our second important goal, Ireland. We found Dingle, and we spent several hours with the sacristan at the local church (the pastor was in Dublin for a horse show!) trying to locate relatives. We had our grandfather's name and also the name of Dennis O'Connor but we didn't have specific enough information to locate any relatives. (O'Connor is a very common name in that part of Ireland.) Our penultimate stop was Belfast where Carol had a "pen pal." I don't remember much about Belfast except that we found it wise to keep the fact that we were Catholics to ourselves.

Last of all we visited Edinburgh in Scotland where we were lucky enough to attend some concerts which were part of the annual Edinburgh Music Festival. Featured that year were Yehudi Menuhin and Pablo Cassels! Carol flew home from there or Glasgow and I journeyed further north to visit a Scottish friend from the Greg named Walter Scott! A highlight of that visit was sailing on the Clyde past Robert Burns' home. Finally I took the train from Scotland to Italy and Rome. How I survived such a ride I do not know, but as George Bernard Shaw said, "Youth is a wonderful thing. What a crime to waste it on children."

CHAPTER VII

BECOMING A CLASSICIST

> He who teaches learns
> more than the students do.
> German proverb

When I returned to Vermillion in December of 1958, the Draft Board notified me immediately that I was going to be drafted. Fortunately I decided to visit my former Latin teacher, Grace Beede, with whom I had studied as a sophomore at USD. The visit went well and much to my surprise, she called me the next day and offered me a teaching fellowship at the U beginning almost immediately, i.e. in January of 1959. I was to teach two classes and work on a M.A. degree. This sounded a lot better than going to the army so I accepted it, and the Draft Board gave me a deferment (which was renewed yearly until I was too old to serve!). This was definitely one of the closest calls of my life. The first day I stood in front of a class, I thought "Wow! This is a real high; this is something I can do!" I had hoped for a long time that I'd find something that "came naturally" to me. I thinking teaching did. Teaching is all about love—love of students, love of learning, love of the subject matter, and love of teaching. I can honestly say that forty-eight years later, when I taught my last class before retiring, I was as enthusiastic about teaching as I was that first day. After earning a M.A. at USD I taught there full-time for four years, 1960-61, 1961-62 and 1964-65 and 1965-66.

Colleagues at USD including Grace Beede told me constantly that I would never get ahead teaching on the college/university level without a Ph.D. Hence during the 1961-62 school year I began examining graduate schools. Everyone expected me to go to California which was a common destination for young people in the '50s and '60s. (A popular gift for South Dakotans when they graduated from high school then was luggage which the graduate would need for the trip to California.) I applied to several universities, and was offered fellowships to U.C.L.A., Wisconsin and Michigan. I chose Michigan because it had the best reputation and because Miss Beede was on good terms with the chair, Gerald F. Else, a native of South Dakota although U.C.L.A. offered me a more generous financial package. Being a contrarian by nature I moved eastward when most of my friends were heading west.

I arrived in Ann Arbor in the fall of 1962. I had been advised by a friend to look up a certain Fr. Johannes who was finishing his Ph.D. I did, and in fact he helped me find a room in the building he lived in, and we became friends. While I was visiting him that first time, a classmate of his dropped in who was schedule to take his final oral the next day. I'll call him Ted. He had been working on his doctorate for many years under the old program (explained below), and he failed the final oral exam! (I heard later that he had been invited back to retake it, and he passed. Whether or not he found a job, I don't know since I never heard anything about him nor did I ever run into him at professional meetings.)

In any case, Ted's failing his final oral had a devastating effect on the morale of graduate students, or at least it did on me. Years passed and no one was finishing the Ph.D. program. I will admit that I was unusually anxious, but I felt that the faculty didn't want anyone to finish. I worried that they didn't think we were good enough. The faculty at Michigan had all done their graduate work at Harvard, Yale, Princeton or Oxford, and they wanted to raise Michigan up to that level. Friends told me it would have been easier for us if we had gone to Harvard or Yale.

The thing I remember most about that fall was how stressed out I was. The Classics Department was inaugurating a new three-year Ph.D. program. (Their old program usually took five or six years to complete.) There were two years of coursework in the new program at the end of which came six written "preliminary exams," each four hours long, one in the history of Latin literature, another in the history of Greek literature, one in a special Latin author, another in a special Greek author, one in ancient history in general, and finally one in a special field such as archeology, philosophy, comparative grammar or whatever. One of these six could be postponed, but only one. Upon arrival we had to pass "qualifying exams" in Latin and Greek. Also before the end of the second year students were expected to pass exams in French and German. Besides all of this there was a reading list which, as colleagues said, Ulrich von Wilamowitz-Moelendorf, perhaps the greatest classical scholar of modern times, could not have read in a lifetime. It might have been possible to accomplish all of this, or most of it, if one didn't have to teach, but in those days almost everyone was a teaching fellow. At least two of the three who started out that fall with me were. I taught two courses, not two sections of the same course, but two different courses namely Elementary Latin and Vergil. (I had some previous teaching experience so I was asked if I minded teaching two courses which naturally meant two preparations and at least six hours in class per week.) Finally we teaching fellows met once a week with Gerda Seligson to discuss pedagogy, linguistics, etc. We were using a Latin text by Waldo Sweet which was entitled *Latin a Structural Approach* which I loved since it stressed oral Latin which was one of my strong points, but it meant practicing asking Latin questions to elicit Latin answers, memorizing "basic sentences," etc.

The three year Ph.D. program was, I believe, the brainchild of Gerald F. Else who was, of course, internationally known for his work on Aristotle's *Poetics* and on the origin of tragedy. One of the years when I was in Ann Arbor he was the president of the APA, the American Philological Association, the leading professional organization for classicists. Else was a master teacher and a brilliant administrator. If I could fault him for anything it would be for having unrealistic expectations of what mere mortals could accomplish in two or three years. I lasted two years, thanks to two of the kindest people I have ever known, Don Cameron and Frank Copley; without their interest and encouragement, I would not have finished the first year. As it happened all three of us in the new program were on the verge of nervous breakdowns by the end of the second year. I took my five required preliminary written exams and left town vowing never to return if I didn't pass. Fortunately I passed, but I taught for two years at the University of South Dakota and then won a Danforth Fellowship (most likely thanks to Grace Beede who had contacts at the Danforth Foundation since she had supervised the planning and construction of USD's Danforth chapel.) This made it possible for me to study full-time in 1966-1967 and work on my dissertation during '67-68. In those days there were lots of jobs. I recall attending an APA meeting in Toledo and getting several job offers while standing around in the hotel lobby. The bottom fell out of the job market, I have been told, in 1969. So this was one of the "close calls" that I'm going to talk about in this memoir. If I hadn't found a position at Macalester College in the spring of 1968, I might not have found a job teaching Classics after all I had gone through to get a doctorate.

One of my classmates had a worse time than I did. There were three of us who started out together on the "new Ph.D. program." One peer was a

Lutheran minister, the other a young lady who had majored in Classics at an elite eastern women's college. I'll call her "Sally." One day towards the end of the second year as we were preparing for the written preliminary exams, I ran into the minister as he was coming from the Mental Health Clinic, and I was on my way to the Allergy Clinic, both of us suffering from stress. He asked me if I had noticed that he and Sally were studying together all the time. I said that I hadn't noticed. He proceeded to tell me that he and Sally had fallen in love and were planning to marry. This meant that he was divorcing his wife, and because of that the church was defrocking him. However, he said this didn't matter since he had lost his faith anyway. And I thought that I was going through a lot! After the preliminary exams were over the minister began working on his dissertation which involved a study of "epithets" in the *Iliad* and *Odyssey*. (Epithets are descriptive words or phrases added to names, e.g. "swift-footed" Achilles, Zeus "who thunders on high," Hector "of the shining helmet.") Since in 1966 computers and copy machines were just becoming available, he had everything on 3 by 5 cards stored in shoeboxes. The chair of the department was directing his dissertation. One day G.S. Kirk who was the Regius Professor of Greek at Oxford happened to be visiting the department, and my friend discussed his dissertation with him. Kirk told him that what he was trying to do couldn't be done in a lifetime. Nevertheless, he continued to work on the project after he found a job at a nearby university.

One day one of his colleagues told him that he should probably keep his shoeboxes with all his research at home since there was concern that radical students might burn down a university building in which case he would lose everything. (This was a real possibility in the late '60s and early '70s.) While he was putting the boxes into the trunk of his car, he dropped them, and the cards were scattered all over the ground. My friend told me years later that he went a little berserk when this happened and began throwing the cards up in the air. He then got in the car and was about to drive away, but his wife insisted that they save the cards, and she threw them into the trunk. A couple of years later, he realized that he wasn't going to get any salary increases, promotion or tenure unless he started publishing. Hence he put the cards back into order and wrote an article which was published in a respected journal. His dissertation director happened to read it and counted it as a dissertation! Thus my friend got his Ph.D. and went on to have a distinguished career at his university.

I am not sure when I got "hooked" on the life of the mind. I certainly was in Ann Arbor, but I had been inspired earlier by the Benedictines, as

I said, and also by the internationally renowned faculty members at the "Greg." I was impressed by scholars and others too who were polyglots and were well read in several traditions. Even as a kid I had thought how wonderful it would be to speak a second and even a third and fourth language. I fantasized about traveling in Europe and being called upon to serve as an interpreter. Besides Latin and Greek I studied Sanskrit and dabbled in Old Church Slavonic, Gothic, etc. for my work in comparative Indo-European linguistics. As far as academic fields are concerned, I loved philosophy most of all and then theology. Although I always loved poetry, I never considered literature my *forte*. In graduate school I realized that many went into literature as a substitute for religion and sought aesthetic experiences to compensate for their lack of religious experiences. I always loved history, but it takes a special kind of mind to be an historian; one much have historical imagination and be interested in politics; in graduate school I had neither. (My interest in politics grew out of my involvement in campus politics at Macalester.) At Michigan I gravitated towards philology, the study of languages and manuscripts.

After earning my Ph.D. I became interested in World War II and especially the life of Hitler and the Nazi period. This was strictly an avocation and had nothing to do with my professional life. I spend several summers reading about the Holocaust and acquired quite a collection of books on that terrible period. This led to a lifelong affection and admiration for the Jewish people. After retirement I became interested in Stalin and the Communists, another indescribably horrible topic. I found that just as saints such as John Paul II and Mother Theresa can inspire one so also profoundly evil people such as Hitler, Stalin, Mao and Pot Pal can paradoxically enhance one's faith in God. The ancient Greeks knew this, and hence they produced great tragedies.

In Ann Arbor I learned a lesson which surprised me and may surprise some readers too. I was working too hard, and it was thanks to some friends that I learned the importance of relaxing, laughing, singing, dancing and just plain "goofing off" from time to time. During the summer sessions we met almost every night around 9:30 at a popular hangout called the Pretzel Bell for beer and conversation. During the school year I fell in with a group of friends from the apartment building where I lived, and we sat together at football games. We used to drink martinis during the games, and we had a hibachi on which we prepared hot *hors d'oeuvres* to go along with the drinks. It was the Dionysian life as opposed to the Apollonian life of study and rationality. Euripides shows us in his tragedy *The Bacchae* what happens to people who neglect the Dionysian side of human nature. I am indebted to many friends who helped bring balance into my life. Of course in this area as in all areas of life moderation is of the utmost importance, as the ancient Greeks never tired of stressing. But I digress, as Max Schulman so wisely used to say.

During the '68-69 school year those of us who had finished our degrees and those who hadn't were asked to fill out a questionnaire regarding how the Ph.D. program could be improved. That proved the cathartic experience I had been hoping for. Michigan quickly changed the program to a four-year one.

Since no one had finished a Ph.D. in Classics for several years, the faculty were finally showing some concern. My best friend on the faculty, Don Cameron, advised me to find a text that needed to be edited and edit it for a dissertation. Such a text would be finite and could be done in a reasonable period of time. Of course, all the famous authors such as Homer, Sophocles, Euripides, Vergil, Cicero, *et al.* had already been done. I had become somewhat interested in ancient medicine after teaching medical terminology at USD. This was a course about Latin and Greek prefixes, suffixes and roots that are found in medical and scientific terminology. While many people might consider this a boring subject, I was absolutely fascinated by it. I also seemed to be able to arouse the interest of students. In Ann Arbor I audited a history of medicine course in the medical school and was dating Dee Farnella who was a professor of nursing. I knew there was a series called *Corpus Medicorum Graecorum* that was being published in Berlin by the Deutsche Akademie der Klasischen Altertums-Wissenschaft. (Call it the German Academy.) Their goal was to publish new editions of all the ancient Greek treatises on medicine. I wrote the editor, a certain Dr. Kollesch. She responded promptly and told me they wanted several works by Galen for their series. I chose the shortest one. It also had occurred to me that there was plenty of work to do in this field and that one could get grants from both the National Science Foundation and the National Endowment for the Humanities for projects in ancient medicine, many ancient medical writers being both scientists and philosophers. Don Cameron had once told me, somewhat facetiously, that when choosing a text to edit one thing to consider was the cities in which the manuscripts were located. The manuscripts for the treatise I had my eye on were in Paris, Florence, Rome and Mt. Athos in Greece. One couldn't do much better than that.

I applied for a grant from the U. of M. graduate school so I could visit libraries in these cities and produce an "autoptic" edition, that is one based on reading and collating the actual manuscripts themselves rather than relying on photocopies or microfilms. (Collating means comparing the manuscripts. Most people know that, if ten people translate a text from a foreign language into English, there will be ten different versions. What most people don't know is that in the case of ancient texts—Latin, Greek, Hebrew or whatever—there are many different manuscripts. The reason for this is that scribes who made copy after copy for centuries inevitably made mistakes. Hence one of the most important things classicists do is collate or compare all the manuscripts that have survived of a certain work, identify the errors, eliminate them, and then try to establish what the author most likely wrote. Only then can reliable translations be made.)

The graduate school awarded me a grant, and so I set out in May or June of 1967 for Paris first of all. I had planned to stay at the Hotel d'Athens where I had stayed once before, but I could not find it. While looking around the neighborhood a gentleman who was leaning out the window of a building asked me if I was looking for a room. I said "Oui" and it turned out that he worked for a small hotel there which had a room available. It was probably Friday since I planned to work in the Bibliotheque Nationale, where the first manuscript I had to read was, the next morning. I went to bed early being somewhat exhausted from the flight and had just fallen asleep when I heard shouting and all sorts of commotion outside my window. It happened that my hotel was across the street from Les Halles, a huge central wholesale market to which farmers brought their produce during the night. As I descended the stairs to check out the scene, I discovered that girls were lined up on the stairs. My hotel was a whorehouse too! The commotion in the street and in the hotel lasted all night so I got very little sleep. Of course, my Irish Catholic upbringing and seminary training plus lack of money prevented me from patronizing the girls.

Next morning I was at the library early at what I thought was opening hour only to find that it was closed on Saturdays and Sundays. Hence I had two days for sightseeing. Monday morning I was at the front door again at opening time only to discover that it was closed because the day before had been Whit Sunday or Pentacost and Whit Monday was a holiday. I was beginning to worry since my train to Berlin was leaving on Thursday, and I had no idea how long it would take to read the manuscript. Tuesday morning I finally got in. The librarian found the manuscript without trouble, brought it to me wearing white gloves, and set it on the stand in front of me. I was ordered not to touch it and to let her know when it was time to have a page turned. I had just begun to read it when the lights went out and an announcement on the sound system informed us that a general strike had been called. All government offices were closing. Buses, streetcars and the subway would be shut down too. Thus I had another day for sightseeing and only one day left to collate my manuscript. Fortunately things went well on Wednesday, and I finished the task by working from opening time until closing time.

From Paris I went by train to Berlin to confer with the editor. The Deutsche Akademie turned out to be in East Berlin, and this was during the height of the Cold War. I will never forget the fisheye stare that the East German border guard with his ugly green uniform and machine gun gave me as I showed him my American passport. At least I knew enough not to carry microfilm with me

The Deutsche Akademie was the most drab and most spartan place I had ever seen. It was obvious immediately that publishing ancient Greek treatises on medicine was not at the top of the list of East Germany's priorities. The editor, though, turned out to be an attractive young lady although not fashionable dressed—the only bright spot in the whole dreary place. Since her English wasn't much better than my German, we didn't have a lot to say to each other. I was invited to lunch with her colleague who could speak English. The lunch consisted of borsch and brown bread, the sort of thing one might be served in the Gulag, and we ate under the watchful eyes of Marx and Lenin. Dr. Kollesch gave me a copy of her dissertation which had been published, but on the condition that I would send her a certain book once I returned home, which I did.

When I finished my dissertation about a year later, I submitted it for publication in their series. I had carefully followed the guidelines, and I had a critical edition of the Greek text, based on all the known manuscripts plus the first translation into English, and an introduction. She then requested a commentary which had not been mentioned before and which I had no desire to do. Hence my dissertation was never published except by the University of Michigan in microfilm form. Years later I learn from others who had prepared similar volumes for the series that theirs were never published either. In fact, as far as I know, the Deutsche Academy didn't publish anything, and their way of stalling was to keep asking editors for more commentary, a longer introduction, or whatever. The fact was they had no money. Hence her request or rather insistence that I send her a book in return for her dissertation. Under communism people were lucky to have enough to eat and a place of some sort to live in. Had I known then what I know now about communism I would never have dealt with them. (What I said about their not publishing anything was true years ago. It may be that since the fall of the Berlin wall and the return of a certain amount of prosperity to eastern Germany, they have published some works.)

From Berlin I made my way to Florence where a wonderful lady who worked at the Laurentian Library found the manuscript I need to read and let me read it. My stay in Florence was uneventful. From there I flew to Greece where I stayed in Athens at the Stanley Hotel which I believe cost one dollar per night. I left Athens by plane, an old DC 3, for Saloniki in the northern part of Greece. It was evening as the plane was taxiing down the runway, when someone burst out of the cockpit and ran down the aisle. Then we heard a door slam. We had been about to take off with a back door open or partially open. It was just the first exciting event in a trip that included many more.

After I checked into my hotel in Saloniki, I went to a nearby bar for a beer. No sooner had I sat down then a pretty girl joined me, and the waiter arrived with an expensive bottle of champagne, cork screw in hand. They apparently thought I was an American soldier from a nearby base. I made a hasty retreat through the nearest exit and found another place for a beer.

At my hotel, in response to my question about going to Mt. Athos, the desk clerk advised me to go to the bus depot next morning as early as possible, for instance 4:30, because there was no bus schedule. I should take the bus marked "Uranopoli," and it would leave whenever it was full. In the station next morning several men approached and spoke German to me. They had learned some German during the second world war when Greece was occupied by the Germans. German was a foreign language for them, and it was obvious that I was a foreigner so it was expected that I could speak German. Fortunately a young man, an artist who could speak English quite well, came over and helped me get a ticket. His name is Manos, and he was going to Mt. Athos to paint scenery and monasteries. We ended up traveling together for several days. We were later joined by a German. Manos and I spoke English; Manos and the German spoke German, and German and I communicated with French. The three of us had no common language, but we got along fine. In fact, I thanked God often for Manos. My trip would have been much more difficult without him. (Footnote I shudder now to think about traveling alone in such places as East Berlin and northern Greece with very little money and with health insurance from the University of Michigan which may not have covered much in Europe. Again GBS's quip about youth being a wonderful thing comes to mind. When the bus was full we left for Uranopoli, the last city before one entered Mt. Athos. I should explain that Mt. Athos is a peninsula in northern Greece inhabited solely by monks. The peninsula is "extraterritorial" in the same way that Vatican City is in Italy. (Vatican City, although surrounded by Italy, is an independent country with its own government, flag, police force, stamps etc.)

At Uranopoli we took a fishing boat that sailed along the southern coast of the peninsula to Daphne where we had to go through customs. (One has to have a visa in addition to a passport to visit Mount Athos.) The first thing I noticed was that all the clocks appeared to be stopped. Then I was informed that the monks told time as it was told in biblical times—the first hour was 6-7 in the morning, the second hour 7-8, the third hour 8-9, and so forth. Also the calendar was different since the monks never accepted the Gregorian calendar, named for Pope Gregory XIII who decreed its use in 1582. On Mt. Athos they were still using the Julian calendar named for Julius Caesar. At the time I thought one would have to go to Tibet to find a more exotic place.

After presenting our passports and visas, signing various documents, etc., we were advised to walk northwards through the forest to the north shore and catch another boat to the Grande Lavra, the last monastery on the peninsula, where my manuscript was located. We were also warned to watch out for wild boars along the way through the forest. I hadn't prepared for such a walk and was lugging a huge suitcase and wearing street shoes while the other two had backpacks and hiking boots. Still I managed to keep up.

Along the way we passed several deserted monasteries in one of which a hermit lived. As we approached him so Manos could talk to him, he noticed us coming and ran off and hid. At another monastery a very talkative monk engaged Manos in a lengthy conversation, or I should say monologue. When he finally stopped, and we resumed our journey, I asked my Manos what it was all about. He said the only thing the monk could talk about was the miracles that had occurred there because of their icons. According to Manos this monk was very childlike and not at all well educated.

Once on the second boat a monk told Manos that the community at Grande Lavra was split into factions, and the members were feuding. He also said that, if the first monk I met belonged to a different faction from the one the librarian belonged to, I would never get into the library.

Fortunately I must have met someone who belong to the same faction as the librarian since I was directed to the library, where I showed the librarian the number of the manuscript I wanted to read. He brought it out, set it on a small table, and pointed to a chair I was to sit in. He sat on the other side of the table watching every move I made, the whole time cracking open and eating pistachio nuts. In spite of the bothersome noise I collated the manuscript in one day.

That evening three Englishmen arrive so I had someone to talk to. They told me that guests could stay on Mt. Athos, going from monastery to monastery, for a week without having to pay anything. After a day or so I began retracing my steps to Saloniki and thence to Athens. I neglected to say that women are not allowed on Mount Athos (or female animals either if what I was told is correct.) Even three or four years ago when The International Association for Greek Philosophy held its annual conference in northern Greece and there was an excursion to Mt. Athos, women were allowed to take a boat ride around the peninsula but could not visit the monasteries or set foot on the their property. I went with the women as a silent protest for their exclusion. It appeared then that many monasteries had been refurbished and that monasticism is flourishing in Greece again.

In Rome on the way home I encountered a wonderful old friend, Richard Luman from whom I had taken Greek history at the USD and whom I had visited several times when he taught at the University of Chicago. We spent a very pleasant few days together. That was 1967, and he had been in Greece when a coup took place—the colonels had taken over. The streets were full of tanks and soldiers, and it was terrifying experience which, thanks be to God, I had been spared since I was with the monks. I then made my way back to London whence I flew to Detroit to prepare for marriage to Dee Farnella.

Before concluding this rather long chapter about my adventures in Ann Arbor, I want to relate an unusual experience I had one summer in a course taught by a visiting professor. Warren Cowgill was a professor of linguistics at Yale and was considered one of the 20th century's greatest authorities on the Indo-European language family. He was also the worst teacher I ever had, or at least that is how I felt during his class. At the beginning of the summer there were about thirty students in the class which was called "Comparative Grammar of Latin and Greek." Most of the students were high school Latin teachers, but three of us were graduate students. Cowgill had absolutely no rapport with the class. He didn't even face the students; he sat on the edge of his chair, looked at a side wall and spoke in a monotone. Each day he would fill the black boards on three walls with conjugations of verbs—first the Sanskrit verb, then, as I recall, the Gothic verb, and then the verb from some other exotic language such as Old Church Slavonic. The students were dropping daily until there were only the three of us graduate students left. We went to visit him during his office hours and told him bluntly that we didn't know what what going on and that we had thought the course was going to be about Latin and Greek. He was surprised. He had thought that we were right with him. He explained that knowledge of these languages was necessary to really understand the relationship between Latin and Greek which he was going to take up the next day. The next day he continued in the same monotone but at least he put paradigms of Latin and Greek verbs on the boards. Only once did he venture to tell a joke. While discussing imperatives, he explained that there are present and future imperatives, but the past tenses don't have imperatives. This, he explained, wasn't a problem since "We don't ordinarily give commands to be executed at a time anterior to the present." He then laughed and laughed. He thought his comment was absolutely hilarious.

On another occasion one of us screwed up his courage to ask a question, something that had never happened before. Cowgill became very flustered and embarrassed and explained that there were examples of that in Albanian, but he didn't know Albanian well enough to quote them. Cowgill was a young man then, but very eccentric. He walked with a shuffle and wore button down shirts that were never buttoned. Once at a departmental tea he came in late, walked across the room in front of the chair who was speaking. He picked up a cup of tea and a cookie, and as he did so, a napkin that had fallen on the floor stuck to his shoe. He then retraced his steps across the front of the room dragging the napkin while the chair was still speaking. He sat in the front row, drank his tea, ate his cookie and promptly fell asleep and snored loudly.

There is a point to this story. Although, as I said, Cowgill was the worst teacher I had ever encountered, the following year I kept thinking about the course. Slowly the relationship between Latin and Greek (and English and many other languages) became clearer and clearer. I read and reread the textbook he had used, memorizing many of the examples. I fell in love with the field and decided to make it my "special field" in the Ph.D. program, and it is a subject I love to this day. (Anyone curious about the Indo-European family of languages should consult the dictionary of I.E. roots and the accompanying article in the *American Heritage Dictionary of the English Language.* Be forewarned, however, that you may get hooked.) Cowgill changed my life. The point is that, although his pedagogical techniques left much to be desired, his vast knowledge inspired at me and no doubt many students at Yale and elsewhere. Good teaching can bear fruit belatedly, and conversely some teachers who may dazzle their students by their performance in the classroom turn out to be "idols with clay feet" upon further reflection. In my own teaching I have always kept in mind a saying attributed to Cardinal Newman: "The teacher's main duty is to inspire." We cannot force students to learn, nor can we learn for them. The best thing we can hope for is that by our scholarship, our enthusiasm for the subject and our love of teaching and learning we will inspire them to want to learn. Courses on pedagogy that are taught in schools of education may have some limited value, but it is mastery of the subject and one's example as a scholar that makes a great teacher, especially on the secondary school level and in college. I know from perusing some journals recently that Cowgill inspired not only many students but his fellow scholars also.

Dee and Jerry with Grace Beede at her retirement party.

CHAPTER VIII

SEVEN LEAN YEARS (1968-1975)

> A liberal arts college is one that
> attracts liberals.
>
> Macalester student

This chapter consists mostly of an interview I gave in 2007 as part of an oral history project at Macalester. In it I discuss how I got a position at Macalester; how the Classics Department barely survived a financial crisis; how "liberal Art" Flemming nearly destroyed the College; how Macalester became a "do your own thing" college; my understanding of liberal arts education; how radicals took over the College; why John Davis is called "the man who saved Macalester; and other professional activities.

What I did not say in this interview is that Arthur Flemming came to Macalester with one idea, namely to start a special program for black students (not minority students, just black students). It was called the "Expanded Educational Opportunities" program, and he persuaded the Trustees to let him take $1,000,000 from the endowment for seed money. He assured them that there would be massive federal funds flowing in once the program was established. He also persuaded the faculty that we should recruit seventy-five students each year for four years to build up an enrollment of 300 E.E.O. students. Each student would receive tuition, books, room, board, travel expenses and an allowance. The package, we were told, would amount to $10,000 per student. The first year instead of limiting himself to seventy-five students, he recruited ninety.

The program was out of control from the start. The administrators Flemming brought in to run the program turned out to be Black Panthers, Black Muslims and other radicals. They said that white faculty were not qualified to judge the abilities of black students so they selected all future participants themselves. Their idea was that we should recruit students "whose high school records didn't show their true potential." If there were kids on the south side of Chicago with outstanding abilities and high school records, let them to go Loyola or the University of Chicago. Hence we ended up with students in some cases who had not even planned to go to college.

Whatever the E.E.O. students and their advisors wanted, Flemming gave them. If they wanted three new counselors, he would chide them for not asking for more. Eventually the E.E.O. program set up its own admissions and financial aid offices. Since some students who were living on campus said that living in dorms was not part of their culture, Flemming let them rent apartments closer to the ghetto (to the extent that St. Paul had a ghetto). Eventually they set up their own African American Institute in the Commodore Hotel which was about half way between the college and downtown St. Paul. There were buses transporting students back and forth. Rumor had it that courses were being offered that had never been approved by the College's curriculum committee. We were told that the "straw that broke the camel's back" was Flemming's granting permission to the E.E.O. students to use one of the College's houses as a "Black House," a sort of fraternity house for them. (Wallace had given the College money to buy nearby houses to prevent the neighborhood from degenerating.) It was the Black House that led the Wallaces to cease supporting the College, and this caused the financial crisis discussed below. Every budget in the institution had been cut, and numerous faculty and staff had been fired, as described below, before the budget of the E.E.O. program was cut in the summer of 1974. That is what led to the occupation of the Administration Building in the fall of 1974. This episode which nearly destroyed the College was caused in my opinion by the fanaticism of Flemming, the naivete of other members of the administration, and the ignorance and arrogance of the majority of the faculty. Flemming thought he had the Wallaces in his pocket and that they would support whatever he did, but he was wrong. Visiting black scholars were shocked by the fact that the administration was initiating a new program of this sort with very little forethought or preparation. The faculty thought we could define liberal arts education any way we wanted to and could call anything we wanted a liberal arts education.

The E.E.O. program was a "commitment," a technical term that had replaced "reason" in the philosophy of Existentialism. While there are rational commitments, this was a leap based solely on emotion. It was a leap into the abyss which nearly resulted in the death of a fine institution.

Interview with Jeremiah Reedy

Laura Zeccardi, Interviewer

August 14, 2007
Macalester College
DeWitt Wallace Library
Harmon Room

LZ: My name is Laura Zeccardi, and I am a new graduate of Macalester College conducting interviews for the Macalester Oral History Project. Today is Tuesday, August 14th, 2007, and I am interviewing Jerry Reedy, Professor of Classics, in the Harmon Room in the DeWitt Wallace Library. Maybe we'll just have you state your name, where you're originally from, and when you came to Macalester and then you can start.

JR: Well, my name is Jeremiah Reedy. I'm a Professor Emeritus of Classics. I came to Macalester in 1968 from the University of Michigan where I was finishing up my Ph.D. in Classical Studies. I was born in Rapid City, South Dakota and grew up in Vermillion.

LZ: And then if you want to start with what you have and then we can go from there.

JR: What I wanted to say first of all is that I'm relying on my memory, so this is a memoir, not a history. I'm not a historian. I did not do research, although I pulled a few things out of my file before the interview today. And the second thing I'd like to stress is that I am loyal to Macalester College and actually very fond of it. It's a wonderful place in many ways, and it's very close to being the institution that I always hoped it would be. It's not perfect, but it's about as perfect as anything such as this can be.

In the Spring of 1968, I was at the University of Michigan in Ann Arbor, working on my dissertation. On the very day that I was to accept a position at a university in Ohio, I got a call from one Lou Garvin, who said he was from Macalester College. I had never heard of him, nor had I heard of Macalester College. He was in Lansing and asked if I would be interested in coming up from Ann Arbor for an interview on that day or

the following day. I grew up in South Dakota, and had always thought that
the Twin Cities would be a wonderful place to live. So I decided to go for
the interview. I called the university in Ohio, and they gave me another
week to make my decision. So I drove up to meet with Dr. Garvin, who
was the Provost of the College. I was very impressed by what he had to say
about Macalester. You might even say I was dazzled by it. The endowment
was $25 million, which was a lot of money in 1968. And the founder of
the *Reader's Digest*, DeWitt Wallace, was pouring more money into the
college. They had some extraordinary fringe benefits for faculty members
such as "faculty foreign fellowships." One could get money to travel or
study in Europe, or I suppose Asia, or any place in the world, during the
summer. New faculty members received a thousand dollars to buy books
for the library in their field, and, believe or not, $300 to buy books for
their own personal library. There was even a babysitting fund. If a faculty
member and his or her spouse went to a College event, the College paid for
the babysitter. So these are not fringe benefits that are commonly found.
Plus, the College owned many houses in the neighborhood which were
rented to faculty members. And finally, Macalester had, I was told, more
Merit Scholars than Harvard. And I'm sure that was true. So the interview
went well, and he told me, if I wanted to visit the campus, to simply
call his secretary and she would get tickets from Northwest, and I could
visit the campus. So I did. Again, the visit went well. I met with several
individuals one by one. And at the end of the day, Dr. Garvin asked me
what the university in Ohio had offered me. I told him and he offered me
ten percent more. What's very unusual about this is that, as far as I know,
the position was never advertised, nobody else was interviewed, there was
no affirmative action or anything of that sort, and I got the job. That was
the spring of 1968. We moved here in August of '68.

I'll mention one other unusual thing, which would upset young faculty
members, or will upset young faculty members if they find out about it. I
was given tenure at the end of my second year on the basis of a half-page
memo, which the chair of the department wrote to Dr. Garvin. I myself was
not asked to provide anything—no documents, no information, absolutely
nothing. That's certainly not the way it's done these days. As you're going
to see, this was one of the luckiest things that ever happened to me. I'm
very fortunate that I got tenure at the end of my second year. I did have
prior teaching experience at the University of Michigan, and also at the
University of South Dakota. So that was 1968, and Macalester was clearly
on a roll.

Now fast forward three years to the summer of 1971. This is a memo or letter from Ken Goodrich, who was the Vice President for Academic Affairs and the Provost of the college. It's addressed to students who were returning in September, and it's dated 7/7/71, July 7th, 1971. What this memo says, under the rubric "The Supporting Staff This Fall," is that "as one part of overall budget reductions required by income projections, there will be a total of 91 fewer full and part-time positions on the support staff. In some cases positions were allowed to lapse as persons retired or left Macalester." "Altogether, 44 full-time and 14 part-time employees have received termination notices." On the next paragraph under "Faculty Reductions for 1972-73," "In regard to the year after next, 1972-1973, the Executive Committee of the Board of Trustees adopted on June 10 a comprehensive plan for reducing faculty personnel expenses by $300,000, below the level during '71-'72. The plan was recommended to the Board by its Education Committee and was based on the report and recommendation of the Ad Hoc Review Committee, composed of six faculty members, six students (each with five-sixths of a vote), and three non-voting administrators. Altogether, there will be 23 fewer full-time equivalent faculty positions in 1972-73" and so forth. And you can see, the list here, one position in Biology, one and two-thirds in Education, two in English, one in French, one in German, half a position in Mathematics, three in Physical Education. The major in Physical Education and Kinesthesiology was eliminated. And then one in Physics, one in Religion, one in Spanish, and three in the Speech Department. So if you add up 91 and 23, this covers 114 positions which were being eliminated during '71-'72 and '72-'73.

The reason this is etched so clearly in my mind—and I am a person who tends never to throw anything away, so I have a lot of these things on file—the Ad Hoc Review Committee, which was known in the vernacular as the "Chop Committee"—you know, chopping here and there—called our department in for a kind of hearing on two occasions. I shouldn't say that, it wasn't the whole department. The chair was out of the country, and my colleague Ted Brooks and I went before the committee twice. The first time we got the impression that the whole Classics Department was going to be abolished. Now, it is true that Classics was underenrolled in those days. As you will see as we go on, it's also obvious why many students were not interested in Latin and Greek during that period. So we thought the whole department was going to be abolished. And everybody on campus did, too. All the faculty members did anyway. The second time we were called in, we were told that one position in the Classics Department would be abolished, and that would have been my position, I assume, because I was the junior member of the department. We had purchased a house in the summer of 1969. My son was born in 1968 so he was three years old. My wife was a nurse, but she believed mothers should stay home with their kids. She was not planning to go back to work, nor was she interested in going back to work. And I was facing unemployment after three years at the college. I should also say that the bottom of the job market in Classics had fallen out in 1969. That was the year after I had two very good offers. So there were no positions in Classics.

The 23 faculty positions eventually devolved, or whatever word you want to use, to I believe 14—"the axed 14," who lost their positions. I also recall—and I hadn't thought of this for a long time—but, there were students on Nicollet Mall with buckets collecting "pennies for professors," trying to save some of these positions. That was not good PR for the college, needless to say. At the last minute, the night before the Ad Hoc Review Committee was to turn in its report to the Board of Trustees, I got a phone call saying that the committee had decided not to violate tenure. All three of us in the Classics Department had tenure, so the Classics Department survived intact, believe it or not. This was a very traumatic experience. Many of the faculty members who lost their positions then never found jobs again in academia. They found other things to do in the Twin Cities. So you can see, we had gone—well the endowment had gone, as I recall, from $25 million to $17 million in three years. And we had gone from, as I described it, "being on a roll," to laying off large numbers of people. So what had happened? The fact is, as I mentioned—and I'm sure he doesn't care if I say this—I interviewed Carl Drake, who had been Chair of the Finance Committee of the Board, and then Chair of the Board. And I asked him if it was true that the college was technically bankrupt, and he said "Yes". We had come to a point where we had restricted endowment, but we didn't have liquid assets and we couldn't borrow money. One member of the Board of Trustees, a wealthy person, had to guarantee Macalester's checks one spring at the First National Bank. Also, returning students one year were required to make a down payment of $500 towards tuition for the following year, so the College could meet the payroll in May or June. Our salaries were frozen, and then they were cut. Then the cuts were restored, and we got in subsequent years increases of—maybe two percent or three percent. This was when Jimmy Carter was president, and we had double-digit inflation. So, believe me, a lot of faculty members were feeling hard up, and wives were going back to work. People were finding grants or jobs for the summer, etc. I always wondered if the College could have gone bankrupt. Mr. Drake said, "Yes, it could." I don't know anything about finances, I but couldn't imagine a college such as Macalester going bankrupt. What would happen? Well now we know what can happen, because Antioch, which was at one time a better known college than Macalester and better established than Macalester and an older college than Macalester, recently went bankrupt and closed. Some at Antioch hope that it'll be closed for two or three years, I suppose during which they will do fundraising and so forth, and they hope to reopen. Imagine how disruptive that will be for students and faculty and staff. According to Mr. Drake, it could have happened here.

So how did we get into such dire straits in such a short time? Well, I blame one person, and that is Arthur Flemming, who was the President. He came in the Fall of 1968, the same year I came. He had been president of Ohio Wesleyan, he had been Eisenhower's Secretary of Health, Education, and Welfare—a member of the Cabinet—and he was before he came to Macalester the President of the University of Oregon. The way it was explained to me was that Mrs. DeWitt Wallace was an alumna of the University of Oregon. She also served on the Board of Trustees there, and she was very fond of Arthur Flemming. She thought he was the "fourth person of the Blessed Trinity." That's my phrase, not hers or Mr. Drake's. And she thought that he would be the perfect person to be president of Macalester College. The president of Macalester at the time was Harvey Rice. I never met him, but the Board made him an offer, a retirement package, which he couldn't turn down. It included income for his wife for the rest of her life, too, and so forth. So he was persuaded to retire, and Arthur Flemming came then in the Fall of 1968. I don't think Mr. Drake would mind if I quote him, because I did ask him if he wanted this on the record, and he said it was okay with him. He called Flemming "a dishonest son of a bitch" and "an arrogant bastard," and said that Flemming was used to spending HEW's billions of dollars, but he found budgets boring. He didn't like to be bothered with budgets.

Once there was a picture in the faculty lounge—in those days we had a faculty lounge—on the bulletin board, and it showed Arthur Flemming waving his hand, and someone drew a string of dollar bills coming from it, and labeled the picture "Liberal Art." He invaded restricted funds. In other words, you know, people make donations to the college for scholarships in, for instance, geology or music. Well, he didn't pay any attention to such restrictions. He would spend funds on his private projects or whatever. At one point I was told that "Liberal Art" wanted Macalester to get into urban housing. There was a retreat for a certain number of faculty members, not everybody was invited, and he was talking about the College building housing somewhere in the inner city of St. Paul. That's a pretty wild idea for a president of a college and for a college to get into. I'm not mentioning names of people who are still alive, except for Carl Drake. I met a judge once at a social event, Judge Otis Godfrey, and he told me that, if Flemming had been president of anything but a liberal arts college, he would have gone to jail. I asked Mr. Drake if it was true that some Trustees thought that Arthur Flemming was mentally unbalanced, and he said, "Yes, that is true." Once I met John Dozier, who was the Vice-President for Financial Affairs, when Flemming was here. I ran into him at the airport, and I told him he should write his memoirs—write a little history of that period. He said, "It would be considered a great work of fiction." People wouldn't believe what was going on. I asked him how long he thought it would take Macalester to recover from Flemming's administration, and he said, "Never. Macalester will never recover." Well, he was wrong, because the College has recovered. Here we are with an endowment of half a billion dollars, and we are, I understand, a "hot college" with thousands of students applying for 500 positions, and we're very selective. We have excellent faculty, wonderful facilities. So we recovered. There's no doubt about that. And what I've said isn't going to damage the College's reputation, or the College in any way. Otherwise I wouldn't say it. It might damage Arthur Flemming's reputation, but not Macalester's.

So we've had four outstanding presidents in the past few years. John Davis came in 1975. And then Bob Gavin, then Mike McPherson and now President Rosenberg. Even Jim Robinson, who came immediately after Flemming was fired, did about as well as anybody could do in the situation. So we've been blessed with good leadership. The Macalester alumni magazine a few years ago had a picture of John Davis on the cover, and it was labeled "John Davis, the Man Who Saved Macalester." It's definitely true. When you think of what's happening at Antioch, and what could've happened here, you see what a great accomplishment it was for John Davis, coming in 1975, to turn the college around in a very short period of time. And I might say something more about that later.

As you'll find out, I'm a person who's very interested in liberal arts education and distribution requirements and things of that sort, so let me say something about the academic side of things here. When I came in 1968, Macalester had typical distribution requirements. All students had to take Freshman Composition. They had to take two years of a foreign language.

A religion course was required, a history course, and then two courses in the social sciences, and two courses in math or hard sciences, and also there was a physical education requirement. These were typical requirements all across the country. Now very quickly all of those requirements were abolished. Flemming said that "The Pursuit of Excellence" was an outmoded slogan, and that it had been replaced by the "Individualization of Learning." Now, the "Individualization of Learning," in the vernacular, became "Do your own thing." So liberal arts education came to be "Do your own thing for four years." There were certain requirements. To graduate one had to pass 31 courses. In those days we didn't have credit hours. Going to Macalester for four years, and taking four courses per term, one would take 32 courses. A person had to pass 31 courses and three interim terms (i.e. January terms), and that was one rule. The other one was that student couldn't take more than 27 courses in one division. So that means you couldn't come to Macalester and take 31 courses in Math and Science, or 31 courses in Psychology and Sociology and Anthropology or Political Science, or you couldn't take all your work in Humanities. So this was to bring in some breadth, but it was pretty . . . vague, and as some of us said, pretty hard for a student to hang around here for four years and not fulfill this requirement. What this meant was that a person could graduate from Macalester and get a BA degree without having ever studied a foreign language, without taking a course in history or philosophy or religion or literature. And these are the sorts of courses that people associate with liberal arts education.

I used to give lectures in a course in Education here, and the instructor called me an essentialist. I was "exhibit one" in the section on Essentialism. So an essentialist, in this context, would be someone who thinks that there are certain courses that everyone who is certified with a BA degree as liberally educated, should have taken. I thought and I still think that there are certain works that everybody who goes to a liberal arts college should read, such as, say, the Hebrew Scriptures, and Homer, and maybe Virgil, and Dante and so forth. So I was labeled an Essentialist. Now what would the opposite be? Well one spring, just before graduation, forty seniors were interviewed by a team of faculty members from the ACM, the Associated Colleges of the Midwest. These students were asked questions such as "What is a liberal arts college?" and "What is a liberal arts education?" One student said, "If this is a liberal arts college, I must have a liberal arts education." Several students said a liberal arts college is one that attracts liberals. Politically liberal, I guess. Most of them said the word "liberal" in the phrase "liberal arts" means that you're free to do your own thing. You can take anything you want to take. I'm probably going to get into trouble, but these faculty members said that the students had apparently never been involved in a discussion of what liberal arts education was. And what I said was that if these interviewers had interviewed forty Macalester faculty members, the answers wouldn't have been any better. We didn't talk about liberal arts education much in those days. Now, the student who said, "If this is a liberal arts college I must have a liberal arts education," I would call an Existentialist. In other words, I am an Essentialist, but the Existential approach to liberal arts education would be to go to a liberal arts college for four years and then at the end look back and say "Aha! That's what a liberal arts education is". You could have ten people who would have nothing in common, and who would all have a liberal arts education because there's no essence in that approach.

Now, it happened that about this same time, some of our colleagues in the social sciences were defining liberal arts education as "self-actualizing." I thought we ought to be able to do better than that, and it happened that I was asked to write a history of the study of the Humanities for a little book on how to teach the Humanities. So I did quite a bit a research, and I discovered that the study of the Humanities can be traced back to the Sophists who appeared on the scene in Greece in the early 5th century B.C. They were people like Protagoras and Gorgias. Because democracy had evolved recently in Athens, there was need for a new kind of education. If you wanted to run for an office in a democracy, you had to be able to make speeches. If you wanted to participate in a debate at the assembly, it behooved you to know something about rhetoric, too. So there was need for a new kind of education, and the Sophists came forth and were offering it. We think of them as teaching rhetoric, but some taught mathematics; they taught political science, they taught religion, theology, all kinds of subjects. Since what they were doing was absolutely novel and had never been done before, there wasn't a word for it in the Greek language. They could have coined a new word, but instead they took an existing word, *paideia*, which had meant "child rearing". They used that as the name of their curriculum. The Romans—I suppose we should say the elite Romans—used to, go to Athens to study philosophy, and then go to Rhodes to study rhetoric. Call it "junior year abroad." These were people like Cicero and Caesar and Pompey. They were fluent in Greek, and they studied in Athens and Rhodes and traveled all over the Greek world. They encountered this new kind of education, *paideia*, and brought it back to Italy. Again, there wasn't a word in the Latin language for it. They could have used the Greek word, which they didn't want to do, so they translated *paideia* in two ways. One was *artes liberales,* the liberal arts, and the other was *humanitas. Artes liberales* means the sort of pursuits that free people engage in, people who have leisure. Before television and radio and so forth, you'd read history or study philosophy or foreign languages, or something of that sort.

So that's . . . liberal arts education; we always say it's liberating, but it's really, etymologically the kind of pursuits that free people engaged in for their own sake. So its not vocational. Then the other way the Romans translated *paideia* was by *humanitas.* They translated it that way because they actually thought, as did the Greeks, that the study of poetry, and drama and history and philosophy, and so forth, had the capacity to make people more humane, that is, more understanding, more tolerant, more compassionate. It doesn't work infallibly, but there is something to that. So what I discovered in my research was that the history of the humanities was the same as the history of liberal arts education, because from the beginning, until quite recently, a liberal arts education was essentially an education in Humanities with some work in the sciences and math and social sciences to provide breadth. Here we were, on the other hand, giving BA degrees to students who might not have, as I said before, ever studied a foreign language or literature on the college level, or history or philosophy or religion.

I thought this was outrageous, but I was a member of the minority. To support my position, I did some research on the history of Macalester. In 1964 there were big changes here. Prior to 1964 Macalester offered two degrees, a BS degree and a BA degree, a Bachelor of Science degree and a Bachelor of Arts degree. The BA degree was for those students who had a liberal arts education. But if somebody wanted to come to Macalester and didn't want to study foreign languages or literature or history or philosophy or wanted to really specialize in science, it was possible to do it, but they got a BS degree. What you could say is that the distinction between the BS degree and the BA degree was deconstructed, not only here, but probably at most places around the country. Everybody got a BA degree.

It's obvious, as you know I'm sure, that the '60s and the '70s were a very turbulent time all across the country. There was the war in Vietnam, and demonstrations and protests and so forth. I recall being told that during the year '67-'68, the year before I came, the big controversy on campus was whether the boys should be allowed to visit girls in girls' dorms on Sunday afternoon for an hour or two, and *vice versa.* And if so, how wide open the door had to be. This was the big controversy in '67-'68. In '68, when I arrived here, and Arthur Flemming too, the radical student movement that had begun at Berkeley in '64, hit Minnesota. Suddenly we had protests and marches and rallies and demonstrations, and students taking over faculty meetings and presenting us with non-negotiable demands, etc. It was a wild and crazy place. But I would say the turmoil at Macalester was not caused by the war in Vietnam or demonstrations against the war. Again, as I said before, I blame it on Arthur Flemming. There was a kind of death wish, and this was something I was just thinking about this morning. There were people on campus who wanted to abolish almost everything that was traditional or ceremonial, like the Classics Department, and required courses, but other things, too. There were faculty members who wanted to do away with Latin honors. You know, you can graduate *cum laude* or *magna cum laude* or *summa cum laude*. They wanted to abolish that. There were students who wanted to abolish caps and gowns at commencement. And actually they were made optional. They didn't want a commencement speaker, so one year we didn't have one. They might have wanted to abolish commencement, I don't know. So, as I was saying, a kind of death wish or something, to abolish all these things that were traditional and had to do with rites and rituals of liberal arts colleges. The yearbook was abolished. Certainly we didn't have homecoming or a homecoming queen or king. There was talk of abolishing exams and grades. You will find this hard to believe. There was a faculty member in the Education Department who talked about doing away with classes. Now, this sounds preposterous. You might think it's a joke, but about that time we had a Classics major who graduated and married a religion major. They moved to San Francisco, where he was going to study to be a Presbyterian minister. He told me he thought he'd be studying New Testament Greek there. So at Christmas time I got a call from them; they were back in the Twin Cities. So my wife and I invited them to lunch, and I was very eager to find out about New Testament Greek and also what she was doing with her Classics major. Well, she had a job, she was playing in a jug band in a bar. And not only was he not taking New Testament Greek, all the classes had been abolished at San Anselmo, the seminary. Each morning, the students would gather in People's Park and decide where they were going to march that day. So the feeling was, he said, that the situation was so urgent that they had to get out and do something, there wasn't time to study. I don't know what this professor of Education had in mind when he raised the subject of abolishing classes. I don't know what the faculty would have done if that had happened, but it apparently happened at least in one place for one semester. At commencement one of those years, Arthur Flemming thanked the students for educating us, the faculty, and the administration. So it was a kind of reversal there, too. There was a lot of talk about abolishing football. That continued over quite a period of time. I am not a football fan. Let's see, next year will be my 40th year at Macalester, and I have only attended one football game. And that was the year that Macalester set a new record for the longest losing streak. Did you know that?

LZ: I knew they had a pretty bad record.

JR: Yes. They set the record, and it was a big event. The national press was here, reporters from *Sports Illustrated* and so forth to see Macalester set a new record. So I went to that game. The thing I remember most vividly, besides the fact that Macalester lost, was the halftime entertainment. Guess what? A guy threw a frisbee to a dog. That was the entertainment. No marching band or anything of that sort. A guy throwing a Frisbee to a dog. In my opinion we lacked the rites and rituals and traditions and mythology and school spirit of an authentic liberal arts college.

Here is something I just ran across this morning, dated February 15th, 1969. This is the consultant's report on a project called the Educational Resources Committee. It was a faculty seminar with some students participating too. What these consultants said here was that "During the last half century there has been a sharp decline in educational interest in theology and the classics . . ." (They could have just as well said religion.) "offset by greatly expanded interest in the social and pure sciences. In such circumstances, a well organized library, the primary purpose of which is instruction, should not only have added the newly wanted materials, but should also have reduced its holdings in the obsolescent fields." So, in other words, classics and religion were considered obsolescent fields, and the social sciences and the sciences were where the action was. This was their report on library holdings: that the library should reduce its holdings in classics and religion. Needless to say, religion at present time is a red-hot subject, and we also have one of the most flourishing and active Classics Departments in the country. Obviously too, the author of the report was a social scientist.

I was a lowly Assistant Professor, and even though I had tenure, I spent most of my time trying to develop courses that would attract students. I wasn't on any important committees during those early years, and I wasn't a part of the inner circle or the establishment or whatever you would want to call it. I heard a lot of rumors, but I didn't know whether they were true or not. Some of these I tried to verify later. But we were told, for instance that students were going to a travel agency over here by the St. Clair Broiler—it was called Delaney/Joyce—and charging airline tickets to the college, and that Arthur Flemming paid for them. There were rumors that students got loans to buy cars and buy stereos, and Arthur Flemming approved of that. There were rumors that students got loans, and were not required to sign promissory notes to repay them. The rumor was around the campus that students would go to Flemming and demand something, say three new counselors, and he would chide them for not demanding more.

The low point of all this came in the fall of 1974, not '71, but '74. In the fall of 1974—I know many Macalester students have heard about this—twenty-one students occupied 77 Macalester Street, which was the administration building in those days, for the first twelve days of the terrm. At the opening Convocation during Orientation week—this was when parents came with their students, the freshmen, first year students—radical students took over the podium, and forced the president, Jim Robinson, to sit in the audience, and presented their non-negotiable demands. They had about six non-negotiable demands. There were students around the campus with walkie-talkies, and it was kind of like a war zone. Convoys of cars would come and deliver supplies to the occupiers at 77 Macalester Street. There were rallies in the football field, and radical leaders came from California and around the country to show support for the occupiers. The students at the rallies were chanting various things, some of which were very obscene, and this upset the neighbors. I lived near Macalester, and when I came in '68, I had neighbors who told me that when their kids graduated from high school they didn't even bother having them apply to Macalester, because they didn't think they would get in. By 1974, these same neighbors were telling me they wouldn't let their kids go to Macalester, even if it were free. So we lost the support of DeWitt Wallace and other donors and alumni and neighbors. A lot of parents, when they saw what was going on on campus, took their kids and left. The enrollment declined, which obviously added to the financial crunch, and there was a total breakdown of community. I remember students coming to me after class, saying, "Whatever happened to this place? There's no school spirit here or anything." Many faculty members came to campus, taught their classes, and went home. There was one year when month after month we couldn't get a quorum at faculty meetings so business wasn't conducted.

We would gather and someone would call for a quorum count, and we wouldn't have a quorum so the meeting would be adjourned. I think it's fair to say that during those years, like '68–'74, faculty members who could find positions elsewhere took them and left. Recently an alumna confronted me during alumni weekend. Because I had been critical of Flemming during a discussion, she said, "Well if you were so unhappy here, why didn't you leave?" And I said, "Well I couldn't find another job." Actually I wasn't . . . well I was very unhappy from '68–'75, but, as I said, when John Davis came, we started getting back on an even keel, and things changed for the better in a short time.

It was during that occupation that students came to a faculty meeting and told us that many of them didn't want a liberal arts education at all. And of course the reaction on my part and some faculty members was "Then what the heck are you doing here?" They wanted courses in urban warfare and guerilla tactics and jujitsu, and things of that sort, rather than traditional liberal arts subjects.

LZ: So when John Davis came into the college, what sort of things did he and other administrators pursue to get the college back to where it is now?

JR: Well, John Davis was the Superintendent of schools in Minneapolis. When it was announced that he had been chosen to become the president of Macalester, a lot of faculty members were very depressed because elite colleges, or colleges that are aspiring to be top national liberal arts colleges, don't generally go to the public school system for administrators. So we were very depressed. But Davis is a very remarkable leader. He changed the mood on campus in one week. He raised the morale of the faculty and the students and the staff. He brought some unity back. Probably most important of all he brought hope. You see, DeWitt Wallace had been giving a million dollars a year to the college, which went right into the operating budget. But even the Wallaces became disillusioned with Flemming, and they stopped those donations. So we lost the support of DeWitt Wallace. One of the best things John Davis did was he win back Wallace. Davis went to New York, met with him. There were certain agreements about avoiding deficits and operating in the black and so forth. And John Davis was able to do that. And so DeWitt Wallace then remembered Macalester in his will—I'm simplifying it greatly—with *Reader's Digest* stock, which, again, I'm not an expert in this at all, but it had never been traded publicly, and nobody knew what it was worth. When it went on the market, it skyrocketed and our endowment went up to a half a billion. Then subsequently it declined before the trustees were able to diversify the portfolio. Still, that's probably how we got back in the black. But, John Davis does deserve to be called the savior of the college. And if you've ever met him you know that he is a remarkable person, very positive and enthusiastic and also, obviously, very savvy when it comes to leadership. So that's, off the top of my head, how it happened.

LZ: What did the tension that developed because of the financial crisis and because of kind of this upheaval of things do? Did it create tension between faculty members in different departments?

JR: Absolutely. As I said, everybody thought the Classics Department was going to be abolished. When we survived intact, there were colleagues in other departments who were very unhappy and very hostile towards us because they had lost a position and maybe a friend, and we survived. And then there were even deeper disagreements about like what is liberal arts education. As I said, a small group of us—you could call us the loyal opposition—thought that we should have a language requirement. And I still think we should have a required course in composition. It would be a very good idea. So some of us thought that it was a mistake to let the students "do their own thing," take pretty much what they wanted to take. All students had to have a major. I didn't say that before. And the major would have requirements. But as far as the work done outside of the major, there was very little structure and basically students could take whatever they wanted to take. And people used to say we needed an advising system with teeth. But advising systems don't have teeth. Advisors can suggest that students take this or take that, but that's it. So there was a big disagreement over what liberal arts education is, and what the college should be requiring.

I guess I didn't say anything about the Interim term. That was also a controversial issue. Macalester was the one of the inventors of the interim term—a one month term in January in which students studied one course and faculty members taught one course, and we were urged to teach experimental and innovative courses. The courses that worked might eventually become part of the regular curriculum. And there were very good courses. I enjoyed the Interim term, but there were also some courses that lacked academic quality. I was on the Curriculum Committee. I said I wasn't on important committees, but I was on the Curriculum Committee. There were student-led courses. If a student could find a faculty member to sponsor the course, a student could offer a course. Suppose you wanted to, with your experience, offer a course on interviewing. If you could get a faculty member to sponsor it, you could teach that course. A group of students came to the Curriculum Committee, and they were calling themselves the New College. There were six or seven students, and what they wanted to do was get in a Volkswagen microbus, and just head south for the month of January. They didn't want to be tied down to an itinerary or anything of that sort because it might inhibit spontaneity and creativity. They didn't want to tell us exactly what they were going to do, other than head south. They would keep diaries or logs, and at the end of the term turn them in for a grade. Interim term grades, I believe, were all on a pass/fail basis. That also encouraged students to try, say physics or something, if they were afraid to try for fear of a bad grade during the regular term. I voted against the so-called New College, but I was on the losing side. They were given permission to do that for their Interim term project.

I remember another young lady who was going to Florida with her boyfriend. He was going to dress like a hippie, and then they would go into places such as a public library. He'd go and sit close to somebody, and she would be off observing to see how people reacted to hippies or people who looked like street people. That was their project. There an Interim term course on pornography. Probably the first course of that sort in the country. And it was offered by one of my friends. The Today Show sent a camera crew and reporter out here to see what was going on. It wouldn't be so shocking today. It was taught by somebody who said he liked pornography. That's what upset the feminists. There was a course on igloo building, and a course called "Cold Behavior" that was a sociology course. Students went around the Twin Cities to see how people behaved when it was extremely cold. And in those days, we had winters when it was often 28 and 30 below zero. The students observed people at bus stops and so forth, to see how they behaved when it was really cold. That course attracted national attention too, otherwise I wouldn't mention it. I had course called Philology for Logophiles. Philology is an older name for linguistics, and it's broader then linguistics because it involves reading manuscripts and so forth. Classicists are called classical philologists, so I'm a philologist. Philology for Logophiles was an introduction to linguistics, and it was a kind of vocabulary-building course. What I was hoping to do was get students interested in Latin and

Greek, and maybe then they would continue the following semester or the following year. Unfortunately it didn't work that way, but I know students took linguistics as a result of my course. Through other colleges, there were courses such as Sailing in the Caribbean. That's a wonderful thing to do in January if you're from Minnesota. There was a popular course, which I'm sure was very academically respectable, called "Biology of the Hawaiian Islands," taught by Jim Smail from the Biology Department. I taught Philology for Logophiles. And my friend Truman Schwartz from the Chemistry Department planned a course called Oenology for Oenophiles. Do you know what oenology is?

LZ: No, I don't.

JR: It's the study of wine and wine-making. So this course was going to involve two weeks studying the chemistry of wine-making on campus, and then they were going to the Napa Valley to visit wineries and do wine tasting. In those days I think the drinking age was 18 so most Macalester students could have gone. For some reason I don't think the course was ever offered. But those were the innovative kinds of courses that were offered during the interim term.

LZ: Why was it then finally dropped? It seems like there were probably some courses that weren't maybe worth the credit, but it did seem like a very, kind of, worthwhile thing.

JR: An unusual thing happened at Macalester. Again there are many people who could explain this better than I can. But, a large number of faculty members were hired between 1964 and 1968, because in 1964 there was curriculum reform here, and I think that was when Wallace started giving money, too. So the faculty expanded, and a large number of people were hired. As a result, a large number of people about my age retired approximately three or four years ago. There have been complete turnovers in departments such as the English Department. You had departments where everybody was pretty much the same age. You mentioned factions and feuds that developed during the difficult times. Those lasted until, let's see. Suppose someone came in '65 and was here, say, 30 years. He or she might have retired in 1995. So those various factions were at the college until that generation retired. It was my impression that the senior faculty members liked the Interim term. But as they were retiring, a large number of new people were hired, who didn't like the Interim term, and who claimed—and this is certainly true—that more was being expected of them, in terms of publishing and research and for tenure, than was expected, for instance, of me, who got tenure at the end of my second year and didn't even know I was up for it and wasn't required to do anything for it. So younger faculty wanted the January term to do research and writing, and they outvoted the senior faculty members who wanted to keep it. The Interim term was abolished when Bob Gavin was president. The teaching load at one time had been three courses one term, an Interim term course, and then two courses the other term. When the Interim term was abolished, the course load, i.e. the teaching load, was reduced, too. It remained at 3-2. It may even be lower now, I'm not sure. So that's how it happened.

LZ: Could we start after the financial decline, because I assume things were probably, you know, a little "hairy" then. But maybe talk about what you specifically taught in the Classics Department, and who else was there with you and just kind of changes, if there have been changes, within that department, from when you started to when you retired.

JR: Well, I have made many very serious mistakes. But at the same time, I've had a very exciting career, a wonderful career. In graduate school, my special interest was comparative Indo-European linguistics. As you may know, one can compare Latin and Greek and Sanskrit and other languages like Old Icelandic, Old Church Slavonic, and so forth, and reconstruct what's called Proto-Indo-European. That's the prehistoric language from which all these languages are derived. It's a very exciting field, a very interesting field. If you want to know something about it, go to the *American Heritage Dictionary of the English Language*. At the end of it there is an article on Indo-European and the Indo-Europeans, and there's a dictionary of Proto-Indo-European roots. So that was the thing I was really interested in graduate school. It did not occur to me when I came to Macalester that it was a subject that I would never teach because this is something that is usually studied on the graduate level.

The first year I was here, I was asked to team teach a course with David Hopper from the Religion Department; the course was called "Athens and Jerusalem." Athens stands for the classical tradition, and Jerusalem stands for the Judeo-Christian tradition. This course had been designed before I came, and I was asked if I would teach it. So I said, "Sure." My undergraduate major was philosophy. So Dr. Hopper and I taught that course for thirteen years, and it was a very exciting course and a wonderful course, in which we compared Greek thought, Greek philosophy and the Bible,—Reason and Faith in other words. That course got me back into philosophy. So I started taking courses at the University. I spent a sabbatical at Oxford where I was in what they call the sub-faculty in philosophy. I spent that whole term doing research on Richard Rorty and postmodernism. Starting in, let's see, 1991, I began going to Greece in the summer for conferences on Greek philosophy. I just got back last week, and this was the 17th year in a row that I've gone to Greece and given papers. Sometimes I attend two conferences in Greece and sometimes give two papers. I've collected one batch of these papers and published them in a book called *In Love with Logos*. *Logos* means reason and language. I have almost enough papers for another book now. I was delighted to be elected one of the honorary presidents of the International Association for Greek Philosophy five or six years ago. So philosophy, for the last twenty-five years or so, has been my main interest. I also was privileged to teach with Henry West for ten years, the last ten years that I was teaching here, in a course called Ancient and Medieval Philosophies. That was a history of philosophy from the earliest Greek philosophers, the Sophists and the Pre-Socratics, through Plato and Aristotle, the Church fathers all the way up to Thomas Aquinas and the Scholastics. That was a marvelous experience. I learned a lot from Henry, and we had a lot of fun in class. In both of my experiences with team-teaching, with Dr. Hopper and Henry West, I didn't agree with either of them on anything. Actually, we disagreed on everything, but we got along fine. I think we exemplified for the students rational discourse, and showed them that it's possible to argue rationally and dispassionately about things, and you don't have to lose your temper or start calling names or anything of that sort. So both Dr. Hopper and Henry West had profound influences on my special interest of philosophy.

LZ: Did you also teach things like basic or elementary Greek, elementary Latin?

JR: Right. We offered elementary, intermediate, and advanced Latin and Greek. Generally we had good enrollments in elementary Latin and Greek. But then it would be down to five or six in intermediate, and some years we didn't have anybody in advanced Latin or Greek. In addition to language courses, we had courses, such as Classical Mythology which I taught for about twenty-five years. In the morning I would teach mythology, and in the afternoon I would teach philosophy. This is Mythos and Logos, one of those famous dichotomies—the difference between mythical thinking and philosophical thinking. Ted Brooks was a colleague for many years. He was interested in both Roman and Greek literature and especially rhetoric. My colleague Bill Donovan was an archaeologist, and he taught Archeology and Classical Art, Greek and Roman Art, and, I think, Medieval Art. When he retired Andy Overman came. Andy's also an archaeologist and is interested in religion. And Joe Rife is interested in everything—he's an archaeologist; he's also a historian, and he does literature in English and the original languages. His wife Mireille is an art historian who specializes in classical art, and she's taught courses here. The Classics Department just before I retired, began teaching Hebrew. Nanette Goldberg teaches Hebrew, which is a classical language. I understand now they are offering Arabic, another classical language, in the our department. So basically we taught language courses and then, you could call them, civilization courses. Bill Donovan taught Greek history, and Ted Brooks taught Roman history. And then we had Classical literature in translation, and so forth.

I could also say that we've had very good students. One of our students who was here, probably in '69 or '70, Jim Benson, just zoomed through both elementary Latin, intermediate Latin, and also Greek. And he went on to Stanford to get his Ph.D. in Classics, where he got interested in Sanskrit. So Stanford let him take his scholarship and go to India to study Sanskrit. I think it was going to be for two years. He stayed four years. He was able to live in India on this fellowship, or whatever it was, for four years. Then he finished his dissertation and was at Harvard for a few years whence he went to Oxford. He's been at Oxford probably for 20 or 25 years. He's their man in Sanskrit. His specialty is Sanskrit grammar, and there are ancient treatises which were written on palm leaves, and he deciphers those and translates them. So he is one of our outstanding graduates. But we've had many graduates, many Macalester majors go to the University of Chicago, to Berkeley, to Princeton, Harvard . . . I've forgotten where else. But top schools in the country and in the world. So we've had very good students. I never complained about the students. Obviously, however, during this period, say from '68 to '75 or so, there wasn't a lot of interest in Classics.

There were several attempts to abolish the Classics Department. There were colleagues who objected to the fact that everything we taught was written by dead white European males. These are the so-called "DWEMs". We have one poem by Sapho, an ancient Greek poetess, one poem. Otherwise, everything we taught in our department was written by Plato or Aristotle or Aeschylus, Sophocles, Euripides, and Menander and Aristophanes and so forth and so forth. We were criticized for that. Actually, I think it was good for us to have to defend what we were doing all the time, because it forced us to examine our assumptions. I think too, that we tried harder. Because students expect courses in dead languages to be boring, we tried to make them exciting. Since Andy Overman, came we have one of the most flourishing programs in the country. As I mentioned, there was an article in *The Chronicle of Higher Education* about our department, because we have around 25 or 30 majors, and lots of students in the languages and other courses, too, now.

LZ: One question I just thought of that's not on the list is, I know the Classics Department is very active in going on digs every summer.

JR: Right.

LZ: Were you ever involved in the planning of that, or the starting up of that?

JR: Well, I'm not an archaeologist, and so I wasn't really involved in that. I mentioned that when I came to Macalester there were these Faculty Foreign Fellowships. So once, I think the second summer I was here, I got one of those. It was $900, which was enough to live for six weeks or so, and I went on an archaeological dig in France. I felt that I should have an experience in archaeology, because it comes up in all the courses that we teach. We're always talking about archeology in mythology or Greek history and so forth. In Classics almost everything is based on archaeology. So I had one experience in archaeology. Bill Donovan took students to Greece to excavate. Andy Overman started taking them to Israel, and Nanette Goldberg is involved in that dig, too. Then Joe Rife got a permit to excavate near Corinth in Greece, and he's taken large groups of students there. So that, of course, is a wonderful experience for a young person or for anybody. And no doubt archaeology has stimulated a lot of interest in our other courses, too.

LZ: I wanted to talk about the charter school, and then also if you've done research and publication.

JR: Right. Well, I mentioned that I did research on the history of the study of humanities. It turned out to be the history of liberal arts education and its origin in ancient Greece. And I've got some publications on that. But I came to think of myself as an educational reformer. I used to write essays for *Colloquy*, which was the faculty newsletter here, about liberal arts education and about what I thought we should be doing, and weren't. By the way, I never accomplished anything as far as reforming the curriculum here or bringing back some structure and distribution requirements. I also got interested in K-12 education and I used to write editorials and letters to the editors about so-called progressive education. Progressive education is the philosophy of education that's generally taught in schools of education, and it's sort of the philosophy of education of the public schools. What the earliest progressive educators, like John Dewey and William Kilpatrick did was reject classical education. They rejected the methods, the goals, and the content of classical education, and replaced it with what some people call romantic notions about little children and education. So probably ten or eleven years ago, a person who wanted to start a charter school in Frogtown but didn't have academic credentials, came to me and asked if I would be interested. This was a person whom I had met in various organizations that were promoting school choice—Citizens for Educational Freedom, and so forth. And he asked me if I would be interested in going in with him to start a charter school in Frogtown. I said "Yes, on one condition, and that is that it have the Core Knowledge Curriculum." The CK curriculum is a very classical curriculum designed by a Professor of English named E.D. Hirsch, and was first described in his book *Cultural Literacy* which came out in 1987. And then subsequently he had another book called *The Schools We Need and Why We Don't Have Them.* So I said to my friend that I would love to be involved if we could have the Core Knowledge curriculum. He said that he had never heard of it. So I gave him the literature, and after perusing it, he said "That's the kind of curriculum we want." This a curriculum in which first graders study ancient Egypt and Mesopotamia. In second grade they study the ancient Greeks. In third grade they study the Romans and generally, too, Latin is offered. And then they study the Middle Ages and Renaissance and so forth. Then in sixth grade there's a review of the whole thing. It's a very traditional, and very solid—it's described as a content-rich curriculum. So Mike Ricci and I went ahead and I was the chair of the founding committee, which became the school board. We planned the school for about two years. There are federal funds and state funds to start charter schools. It opened probably eight years ago and it was a huge success. It now has about 350 students in K-8. We started with K-3, then each year would add one more year. Much to our surprise, the first year about 75 percent of our students were Hmong. We hadn't planned a school for Hmong, but partly because of the neighborhood, and the fact that some Hmong parents felt that their kids were lost in big schools with a thousand students or whatever, about 75 percent of our students were Hmong. That dwindled as the student body increased to 65 percent. The other 35 percent are minority students, too—black and Hispanic. And I don't know if we have any Caucasian students there at all. I'm no longer involved in that school.

When I retired three or four years ago, I was thinking: "What am I going to do now?" The college is very kind and generous to us emeriti faculty. We have cubicles over in the Lampert building, with computers and access to the help desk and so forth. Actually I have two cubicles—like a little office. I come to my office every day. So, I was wondering, "What am I going to do?" I thought, "Why not try to start another charter school?" So, by this time companies had evolved which would help people who wanted to start charter schools. They would help a person write proposals, get federal start-up funds, etc. So I got together a group of college teachers and friends, and we worked with a company called School Start and we got a charter. We got federal funds. We found a wonderful building in Bloomington, which had been a public school, and was purchased by a church, Cedar Valley Church, which only used it on Sunday morning for Sunday school and Wednesday nights for special classes. So we were lucky enough to find the perfect building. We called it the Seven Hills Classical Academy and it opened last year. Well, we were hoping to recruit 140 students for K-3. We ended up with 257 confirmed registrations! We had to add a third section of kindergarten, and we had a fourth grade and fifth grade. Now every grade is full and we have a waiting list of about a hundred. So it is a huge success. We have an outstanding principal. Everything worked out, and it's taken on a life of its own. It was very stressful and the work was very difficult during the planning period. But once we hired the principal, my job got much easier. There are a million things to do when you start a school. But the burden shifted from the school board to the administration. And so it's a huge success. We were going to offer Latin in kindergarten, first grade, second grade, third grade, but when we added fourth and fifth grade we decided it would be more appropriate for older kids to study Latin. So we have Spanish in kindergarten, first, second, and third grade, and Latin in fourth and fifth grade. My dream is to get someday to the seventh and eighth grade and have Greek offered in seventh and eighth. It's one of the most satisfying things I've ever done, and something I'm very proud of and also very grateful for. The Chinese have a saying: "It's better to light one candle than curse the darkness." Seven Hills is a candle that is burning brightly out there in Bloomington.

LZ: Do you have anything that you're currently working on now?

JR: As far as the school is concerned, I had two goals. One was to do what we're doing in Frogtown—to give a very special education to certain kids, who wouldn't otherwise get it. You know, the kind of education that's offered in elite prep schools where the tuition is $20,000 a year or so. We're doing that, but I'm also hoping that student achievement at these schools will show that this is the best way to educate almost everybody. I hope that these schools will be models for the state and the whole country.

As far as research, once I started going to conferences in Greece, I had a set of deadlines. For example, February 1st one has to have an abstract for the paper for the following summer. They have conferences every summer, so the deadline for the abstract is February 1st. Then on May 15th or so you're supposed to submit your paper. Most people don't make that deadline. Instead we go to the conference, we give our papers, and then the deadline is September 30th to turn the paper in for publication in the proceedings. So this gave structure to my research life, by having these deadlines. Some years there were two conferences in Greece. So I have 19, probably, maybe a total of 24, 25 papers that I've given on Greek philosophy since 1990. Before that I wrote things on liberal arts education and philosophy of education. So I'm doing several things at the moment. I'm preparing the paper I gave a couple weeks ago for publication. I'm already working on the topic for next year. By the way, the topic for the conference in Greece I just attended, and this is the International Association for Greek Philosophy, was one that I suggested a year ago. The topic was "*Paideia:* Education in the Age of Globalization." So I gave the opening paper at the opening session, which was a real honor, too. I will revise that slightly to be published in the proceedings. The topic for next year is the relevance of Greek thought for contemporary issues—a very, very broad topic. I'm already working on my paper, that is, I'm already collecting literature on the topic. As I said I've been to conferences in Greece every year for seventeen years in a row. About half of these conferences have been on the island of Samos, where the organizer has a summer home. This is a very beautiful island in the Aegean, one mile from Turkey. The other years we've met at different places. For instance, when the topic was Philosophy of Medicine, we met on the island of Cos, which was the home of the Hippocratic School of Medicine. When the topic was Philosophy and Art we met on the island of Lesbos, probably because of Sappho. It was art in general. Twice we've met in Macedonia near Aristotle's birthplace. One summer we met in Athens on the site that archeologists think was where Plato's Academy was. So I have papers on philosophy and medicine, philosophy and art, philosophy and religion, faith and reason, and so forth. I've had about thirty papers published in the last twenty years.

I work in both Medieval Latin and Greek philosophy. My collaborator from St. Thomas asked me about ten years ago if I would be interested in helping him translate a work by a Spanish Jesuit named Suarez. And so we translated a work; it's not a very exciting work. The book is entitled *On the Formal Cause of Substance*, and it was published by Marquette University Press in their series Medieval Latin Works in Translation. Now we're doing the footnotes for another volume, and this one is on a more interesting subject. This is Suarez's commentary on Aristotle's *De anima (On the Soul)*. And in a way it's a marvelous thing because it unites my knowledge of Latin, especially Medieval Latin and scholastic philosophy of the Middle Ages, with Aristotle and Greek philosophy. So we have about 120 footnotes left to do and then this will be completed. Earlier we translated another work which was entitled *On Uncreated Being*. It was Suarez's arguments for the existence of God. We were 99% done with that when it got published by somebody else. That can always happen.

LZ: Yeah, that's a tragedy.

JR: In any case, for the last twenty years I've been involved in research in Greek philosophy and medieval interpretations of Greek philosophy.

LZ: Well, I only have one last question and I'd like to close with it and you can interpret it as you want, but I'm curious if you have a favorite memory or fond time of Macalester, or favorite class, or even just kind of a reflection on your years spend at Macalester.

JR: I suppose my favorite classes were ones I team taught, Athens and Jerusalem with David Hopper and Ancient and Medieval Philosophies with Henry West. Those were really outstanding experiences and opportunities. I have lots of favorite students. Basically what I tell people, and I may have said this before, is that one might think teaching dead languages would be boring, but I have had a very exciting career. It couldn't have been better. That's probably it.

LZ: All right. Thank you very much.

CHAPTER IX

ON SABBATICAL AT OXFORD

I saw the spires of Oxford
As I was passing by,
The grey spires of Oxford
Against a pearl-grey sky.
Winifred Mary Letts

Justin Gosling is an expert on Plato who taught at Oxford. In 1985 he had been a visiting professor at Macalester, and I audited his course. In 1996 when I had a sabbatical leave, we decided to spend it at Oxford, and I wrote Gosling telling him I was the guy who audited his course at Macalester and that we were coming to Oxford for Hilary Term. After an initial misunderstanding caused by the fact that Americans and English are "two peoples separated by a common language," as some wit has put it, (Gosling thought an auditor was someone from the business office who was checking on the number of students he had had at Macalester), he helped me get visiting scholar status at Oxford and an appointment to the "sub-faculty in philosophy." (The meaning of "sub-" was never explained.) He had become the head of St. Edmund Hall ("Teddy Hall") after returning from Macalester.

Some weeks after we arrived in England, he called and said there was an American pianist who was performing at Oxford and he would like to have us come to a dinner party and meet her. Naturally we were eager not only to meet her but also to see the interior of his apartment which was part of a building that must have been built in the 16th or 17th century.

We arrived at his front door on the appointed evening. Gosling was waiting for us and reported that the pianist had become ill at the last minute so he invited two of his friends to join us instead—Lord Raymond Plante and his wife, Lady Catherine. Lord Raymond was a member of the

House of Lords and also president of one of the colleges at Oxford. Gosling told us not to worry—I wouldn't have to bow nor would Mary Ann have to curtsy. Furthermore, he informed us, Americans weren't expected to know how to act when consorting with aristocrats. During the first round of introductions it was "Lord Raymond," "Lady Catherine," and so forth, but the second time around it was "Raymond" and "Catherine," so we were on a first name basis with a members of the English aristocracy. Actually they were extremely nice people who seemed genuinely interested in what we were doing. There was also a fourth couple a physician and his wife who were likewise very congenial. The only untoward moment occurred when Mary Ann heard one person asked another if she had "a good recipe for jugging a hare." That was the first indication we had that we were eating rabbit. It was served in a rich brown gravy, and I can confirm the common notion that "it tastes just like chicken."

Other recollections of Oxford—life is very leisurely there at least for the faculty. One weekday Gosling and his wife invited us for lunch. It began in their apartment with sherry in front of the fireplace; then we joined some of his colleagues in the faculty dining room where we had wine with our lunch. No one was in a hurry. Following lunch we repaired to the drawing room for coffee and after dinner drinks. (At Macalester I usually worked as I ate lunch, and certainly I never had wine with lunch or spent two hours at it. I had trained myself from early in my career never to waste a moment. For instance I even put everything important on 3 x 5 cards which I studied while walking which was my chief, even sole, form of exercising for years. Even in retirement I am a fan of "multi-tasking.")

Another vivid memory from our days at Oxford is of the Bodleian library. During the first visit one must take an oath which can be taken in English or Latin. Naturally I chose the latter, and I found myself promising not to light fires in the stacks, not to damage the books and, if my memory serves me correctly, to leave my bow and arrows in the vestibule. Finding a book could be a challenge at Oxford. Part of the collection was catalogued on computer, another part was in the card catalog, and the third part was written by hand in huge books dating from the Middle Ages.

Another difference: at Macalester and earlier at the University of South Dakota and Michigan I was a friend of all the janitors. (It pays to befriend the janitors if you want good service.) At Macalester where I was always the first faculty member on campus in the morning, I was popular with the cleaning staff who worked nights because, when they saw me coming they knew it would soon be quitting time. At Oxford, however, because of the English class system, janitors don't associate with professors, and all my attempts to make the acquaintance of the janitorial staff were rebuffed. The janitor in the philosophy library, in fact, used to run and hide when he saw me coming.

Weekends were spent in London visiting museums, art galleries, historical sites etc. One week and we bought a package tour to Paris which included a train ride through the Chunnel and a stay in one of the world's smallest hotel rooms. The room was only slightly larger than the bed. The only chair in the room was a folding chair, but there wasn't room enough to open it up. The radiator was high on the wall since there wasn't space on the floor for it. The bathroom made airplane bathrooms look spacious. Anyone sitting on the stool would have his feet in the shower. We had a balcony that was all of four inches deep—just large enough for a bottle of wine. I visited other similar hotels in the *Place de la Republique* where our hotel was looking for larger accommodations only to discover that some hotels had more impressive lobbies but the rooms weren't any larger.

At Oxford I followed my usual schedule—rise early, work at home until it was time to set out for the library, arrive there as it opened and then work until noon. I always went home for lunch and a nap. Most of my time there was devoted to a study of Richard Rorty which was part of a larger study of "postmodernism." I set out to read everything written by Rorty, and I think I succeeded. Postmodernism had attracted my attention because I saw it as a rejection not only of the Enlightenment, as is commonly said, but of the whole of Western rationalism which had come to us from the Greeks. The fruit of that study was a paper entitled "Postmodern Art and the Rejection of Reason." It was delivered in Greece at a conference on the island of Lesbos in 2000 and published in the proceedings of the conference.

While I was gone in the morning, Mary Ann painted and made some very attractive sketches. In the afternoons we often attended lectures and visited Oxford's museums and art galleries. There were also lectures in the evenings and sometimes concerts. Mary Ann also joined the "New Comers' Club" which in the U.S. would be called the "Faculty Wives Club." They met for lunch, made excursions into the Cotswolds and visited various historical sites. We also contacted a former student, Jim Benson, who teaches Sanskrit at Oxford. He and his wife entertained us at dinner, and we reciprocated with a dinner party at our rented house. All in all it was a wonderful sabbatical, and we returned to Minnesota rested, inspired and reenergized which is what sabbaticals are for.

CHAPTER X

WIVES AND KIDS

If every parent had children like mine,
the troubles of this world would melt away.
J.R. adapted from Yuval Levin

When I arrived in Ann Arbor in the fall of 1962, I lived alone in what the landlord called a studio apartment, i.e. one room with a kitchenette, bathroom, and a hide-a-bed. It was great for studying, but I wasn't meeting people, making friends, or having any fun. Hence, after a semester or so I began looking for an alternative. I saw an ad in the University paper saying three guys in a luxury two-bedroom apartment were looking for a fourth person to share their quarters. I called and was invited for an interview. They liked me, and they appeared to be congenial so, not having a lease, I moved immediately. It was a very nice large place, the only drawback being that I had a roommate, but the advantages far outweighed that disadvantage. We took turns shopping, fixing meals, cleaning, etc.

The best feature was that there were many graduate students and young professionals in the building which meant that there were parties almost every weekend. This is how I came to know Dolores, Sandy, Marcia, and Dee who shared an apartment one floor up. This was the group that bought tickets for football games for themselves and friends. Soon I was one of this group, as mentioned in a previous chapter. Dee attracted my attention immediately. She was shy and quiet, but I was impressed by her education—a nursing degree from the University of Rochester, a BA degree from D'Youville College in Buffalo, New York (after getting her nurse's certificate she wanted a liberal arts education), and a master's degree from Columbia University. I was also impressed by the fact that she was an assistant professor in the School of Nursing at the University of Michigan.

She was of Italian descent, and I had never dated an Italian girl before, and since I had spent two years in Italy, we had lots to talk about. Suffice it to say that we began dating although I never expected it to become serious.

I will confess that I had been profoundly influenced by Erich Fromm's *The Art of Loving*. It has nothing in common with Ovid's more famous *Ars Amatoria*. Fromm's book contains, on the contrary, common sense notions regarding love from a psychologist. He points out that in many cultures romantic love is considered a form of insanity. He thinks that a person who is infatuated is not in a position to make decisions that will affect the rest of his or her life. Love, he thinks, should involve a rational decision, and it will grow through the years as a couple works together, suffers together, and dreams together. He thought that waiting around hoping to suddenly fall in love was as dumb as a person who sits in front of a canvas hoping to suddenly paint a masterpiece. True love requires hard work and practice. Influenced by these notions, I eventually decided that Dee would make a good wife and mother (and she did!) although we were certainly not madly in love. I confess too that I had noticed in Italy how strong the families were and how good Italian girls were at being "La Mama." Hence, it must have been early during the 1966-67 school year that we began talking about marriage.

Eventually I was invited to meet the folks. The Farnellas lived upstairs in an old duplex which was definitely in the "Little Italy" section of Jamestown, New York although it wasn't actually called that. The downstairs of this duplex was vacant and had been for many years—ever since Grandma Farnella had passed away. It was preserved as a shrine of sorts. Mrs. Papa lived next door, and Benny Munella lived across the street. Aunt Rosie and her retarded daughter Carmella lived one half block east, and next to them was one of Dee's Uncle Tonys. The rest of the clan wasn't far away.

Joe, Dee's father, had a mustache and could have played the godfather in any mafia movie. He always had a new car and a big one, usually a Pontiac. Also be dressed like a millionaire or a mafia don. It was important in the Italian community to cut a *bella figura.* His main job was operating a machine in a factory that made ball bearings. Evenings he worked as a bartender, and on weekends he managed a nightclub. Santa, Dee's mother, worked as an inspector in a furniture factory.

Their parents had emigrated from Sicily and Southern Italy after being recruited to work in the coal mines of Pennsylvania. Families lived in company houses some of which had newspapers on the walls instead of wallpaper. They charged food and other necessities at the company store during the month. On payday the husband's check would sometimes cover the bill, and sometimes it wouldn't in which case the bill was carried over to the next payday. Working in coal mines must be not only the dirtiest job in the world but one of the most dangerous. My father-in-law told me that he remembered when the siren would go off after an explosion or cave-in, and all the families would rush to the entrance of the mine to find out who, if anyone, had been killed. In spite of the tragedies and the hardships, the Italians were generally happy, and alcoholism was not and is not today a serious problem. They were able to cope, I believe, because they had a rich culture—they had a beautiful language; they had all sorts of traditions and myths and rites and rituals; they had their festivals and celebrations, and they had strong family ties. Every Friday there were spaghetti dinners with tons of food and lots of wine and singing and dancing. Saturday afternoon families used to listen to operas broadcast from Canada. (Opera was not originally the "highbrow" entertainment it is today; it was part of popular culture. Even today in Italy one hears ditch diggers singing arias and taxi cab drivers praising their favorite tenor or soprano. In the case of the Irish, on the other hand, their culture was almost totally destroyed by the English who even tried to prevent them from learning to read. The Irish retained their faith but not much else.)

Food was very important in the Farnella household. We were either shopping, planning meals, preparing meals, eating, or reminiscing about memorable dishes or meals. I usually went with Joe to buy the groceries. We had to go to one store for meat because Joe knew Carlo the butcher would give him the best cuts. Then we went to another store for vegetables because Luigi was a friend of his, and we'd get the freshest produce, and so forth. Both Dee and her Mother were *virtuosi* in the kitchen. Both collected recipes, and even in her eighties Santa was trying new ones. Fixing meals involved elaborate rituals. Making tomato sauce took a whole day requiring much stirring, tasting, adding spices, garlic, etc. at just the right moment. Oregano had to be rubbed between the thumb and forefinger before being added to anything. During meals we often talked about how much spaghetti Uncle Tony had eaten at such and such a picnic. None of the Farnellas drank wine, but they always served it to me and Betty who was the wife of Dee's brother John. Since Joe didn't eat chicken or turkey, spaghetti was served at every meal. (This reminds me of the one Italian word my kids learned from their grandparents, "*skiviati*" which must be Sicilian or Calabrese for "to find a certain food nauseating." Their grandfather *skiviated* chicken. We still use the word now and then.) There were special menus for special days. For instance, on Christmas after midnight Mass all the relatives came to the Farnella's for Italian sausage. For a wedding there had to be homemade cookies. Before our wedding Santa and her friends spent weeks, maybe months, preparing hundreds and hundreds of little cookies.

It would take a Dickens or Dostoyevsky to describe Santa, Dee's mother, adequately. A line from Anouilh's *Antigone* comes to mind: "She doesn't think; she only feels." Santa would have funny feelings regarding this or that. Since feelings are always ambivalent, no matter what happened she was right. She once said to me, "It's a sin to be superstitious, isn't it, Jerry?" and I said, "Yes." She then proceeded to explain the evil eye to me, something she not only believed in but had a prayer to cure. Breaking a mirror was sure to bring seven years of bad luck, and one never opened an umbrella in the Farnella house.

After supper the first time I visited the Farnellas, I was left alone in the kitchen with Joe and was expected, I learned later, to ask for his daughter's hand in marriage. Instead we spent the whole time talking about horse racing. I had worked one summer at a racetrack, and Joe had been an avid fan of the sport in his youth. The rest of the visit was uneventful. I was introduced to all "the Blood" which means the relatives, many of whom were colorful characters right out of a Fellini movie. Apparently they liked me especially since I could still speak some Italian, although the Sicilian and Calabrese dialects they spoke differed considerably from the *lingua dei libri* which I had studied.

In Jamestown at that time there were two kinds of people, "doctors and non-doctors" (besides Italians and non-Italians). "The Blood" liked the idea that I would someday have the title "doctor" although I don't think anyone knew what a Ph.D. was. Santa had only finished eighth grade, but she thought she had acquired a good education by watching soap operas. Joe had even less education. Early in the century boys often had to quit school and go to work to help support the family, and it was most likely thought the girls didn't need much more than a grade school education.

Back in Ann Arbor Dee and I began planning the wedding. I wanted a small private ceremony at the Newman Center in Ann Arbor, and she seemed agreeable to that. On weekends, however, she would drive home and come back with different ideas. At first she told me her folks wanted us to be married in Jamestown, but it would be a small ceremony. I gave in, but said I didn't want a wedding dance or anything of that sort. I reminded her that I was a graduate student living on a Danforth Fellowship. My mother had passed away two years before, and my Father was up in years. After the next weekend trip, she informed me that her Father wanted some music at the party after the wedding, may be just a pianist. Again I gave in. Suffice it to say that during each weekend visit plans grew more grandiose until we had a banquet and dance and full dance band. Our wedding turned out to be an Italian version of "My Big Fat Greek Wedding" with I can't remember how many guests—two or three hundred. The good news was that everyone not only gave us a present, but at the dance there was a wishing well, and guests came with envelopes full of money for us. The bad news was that Benny Munella rolled up his pant legs and using a broom as a baton led the guests in the wedding march. Some of my relatives who had never been to an ethnic wedding said it was the best time they had ever had in their lives. Three of my best friends, Fathers Larry Seubert, Paul Kaiser, and Dave Hyman conducted the ceremony which included a dialogue between Paul and Larry about Dee and me instead of a sermon. Later at the dance, Larry, who was getting ready to leave the priesthood, got up on the stage and sang "I'm in the Mood for Love" which shocked the ultra conservatives.

I soon learned that in the Italian community in Jamestown things had to be done in a certain way and no deviations were allowed. Sometime after the honeymoon I began hearing about all the things I had done wrong—both sins of commission and sins of omission. My only defense was ignorance. I told Dee I didn't know anything about "wop weddings," and nobody told me I had to do anything but show up. For our honeymoon I wanted to go to Montréal for the World's Fair so the trip would be an educational experience. In Jamestown the tradition was to go to Wasaga Beach in Canada. Hence we stopped there on our way north to a nice resort hotel. Wasaga Beach turned out to be a third rate, rundown amusement park that had seen better days decades earlier. Even Dee was disgusted by it.

Each day on the honeymoon Dee had to call her mother who would say over and over "Oh Dede, you won't believe what happened," but she wouldn't give any details. Gradually the truth came out. Dee's brother John and his wife Betty were on the verge of divorce even though Betty was pregnant. She must have been told, or else she divined that Larry was planning to leave the priesthood. In any case she apparently fell madly in love with him and chased him all over town. Paul was doing his best to keep them apart by trying to get Larry out of town. Seeing what was going on, John drank too much and passed out or just fell asleep in the priests' motel room. My brother Joe, who happened to be at John and Betty's house when she left in pursuit of Larry, got stuck babysitting and missed much of the fun. When Betty's baby was born several months later, she named her "Hillary" which was Father Seubert's real name, Larry being a nickname. This was the final straw for John so he divorced Betty after a bitter and expensive legal battle.

Larry and Paul were both eventually laicized. Larry married a former nun and moved to San Francisco where they found good jobs and got rich in real estate. Paul also married a former nun and moved to Montana where they raised their family and had successful careers in education. Dave Hyman is still a Franciscan friar and is the Newman Club chaplain at the University of Georgia.

Dee appeared to be completely dedicated to the nursing profession. She subscribed to professional journals and read them. She had been involved in various research projects. Her job was not only to lecture to nursing students but also to supervise them in hospitals. Her knowledge of medicine was awesome. I assumed she would work for a few years or at least until I found a position, but I was wrong. Immediately after the honeymoon she began talking about quitting her job and becoming a mother. She said she hated teaching at the University of Michigan. I should have asked her folks to intervene. She would have listened to them, but she would not listen to me. They had lived through the Great Depression and knew what it was like to be poor. In an earlier chapter I described what I did for my dissertation. It consisted of the collation of manuscripts I read in various cities and on Mount Athos, the establishment of the Greek text, the translation of it, and an introduction. I had done almost all of it by myself since my dissertation director had become nearly blind. There was no guarantee that it would be accepted by the committee nor that I would pass the final oral exam. I was still typing on it on my Greek typewriter. Also in December of 1967 we had attended the annual meeting of the American Philological Association, commonly known as the "slave market," where newly minted Ph.D.s looked for jobs. The market appeared not to be as good as had been reported, and I had only a few interviews. Nevertheless, Dee resigned her position before I had one, and in January she announced that she was pregnant. Thus began one of the periods of anxiety referred to earlier. We should have discussed this before we were married. This was another of the close calls from which I got the title for these memoirs.

Fortunately Divine Providence was watching out for us, and the offer came from Macalester sometime during the early spring of 1968. It was a one or two-year offer contingent upon my reception of the Ph.D. degree.

On the day of my final oral exam there was a huge snowstorm in Ann Arbor, and one member of the committee, who was not well known to me and whom I feared most, was unable to make it to campus because of the storm. He was an M.D. from the school of medicine who probably would have been surprised to learn that my dissertation dealt mostly with manuscripts and Greek grammar and textual problems and problems translating ancient texts into modern English. He taught a course in the history of medicine, and his questions could been very different from those of the members of the Classics Department. Thank God for the snowstorm. After the oral exam, which was open to the public although no spectators attended, the chair emerged from the exam room and was the first person to ever call me Dr. Reedy.

The actual move to St. Paul took place in August of 1968 and was uneventful until we got to the house I had rented. The movers packed for us in Ann Arbor, carefully handling some of my old furniture which I had purchased at K-mart and carefully placing pictures of the sort graduate students have into boxes that were worth more than the pictures. Once everything was in the truck, we were told by the movers to drive as fast as we could to St. Paul. We had to be at the house before they were since they were on their way to Seattle and were just making a brief stop in St. Paul. Earlier in the spring I had gone by train to St. Paul to look for a house. Macalester at that time owned approximately seventy-five houses around the campus which were rented to faculty and students. I picked out a bungalow-style house on the corner of Snelling and Fairmont just across the street from the campus. The current renters of it assured me that they had been perfectly comfortable there and that it was a nice, quiet neighborhood.

Dee and I managed to beat the movers to the house. She took one look at it, and said she wouldn't live there. (Apparently she was expecting a mansion.) While we were debating what to do, the moving van arrived. When told that she didn't want to move into the house, one of the men said, "Listen, Lady, we gotta get to Seattle. If you don't want your furniture moved into the house, we will leave it on the lawn." So we moved in. The first problem that it was very hot so I borrowed a window fan from a neighbor who had come over to welcome us. The second problem was noise from the traffic. In August of 1968 Highway 94 had not yet been completed so all truck traffic was sent southward via our street, Snelling Ave. In addition there was a stoplight a block south of our house so that the trucks began braking in front of it. We discovered the first evening that, if there was traffic, we couldn't hear our TV, and if there wasn't any, the TV was too loud. Also if we shut the windows to keep the noise out, it was too hot; if we opened them, it was too noisy. The next day we began looking for an apartment.

It's hard to believe now but in 1968 many landlords would not rent to couples with children or couples with children obviously on the way. Dee was in her eighth month. After a day of being turned away from place after place, we would decide to stay where we were for semester or so, but once back in the house we found the heat and the noise unbearable. Finally we found a two bedroom apartment on St. Paul Ave. about a mile south of the College. By that time we were half packed and half unpacked. I had to pack up and rent a truck. Fortunately a colleague from Macalester came over to help us, and we moved to the apartment.

On Friday the 13th in September of 1968 I came home from the College at noon and Dee informed me that "her water had broken." She didn't seem overly concerned, and we set out for the University of Minnesota Hospital. When we arrived at the desk in OB/GYN and reported what had happened, the nurse exclaimed, "Why aren't you in a wheelchair?" When the doctor examined her, he said that the baby was in distress, and he was doing an emergency cesarean. Jerry Sean was born with a bilateral pneumothorax which, I was told, meant that there was air outside both of his lungs. When I saw him for the first time, he was breathing as if he had a bad case of hiccups. The resident told me that he had only a 50/50 chance of surviving over night. Fortunately the staff on duty knew what to do. Two tubes were inserted, one on each side of his chest, and the out-of-place air was sucked out. By morning he was a healthy and happy little boy breathing normally. I had spent much of the night in the nearby Newman club chapel praying and crying. Dee came home from the hospital before he did, and Santa came to help take care of both of them. When it came to raising children, Dee seemed to know instinctively exactly what to do. (This is a good place to say that, although I may have sounded critical of the Farnellas above, they were actually very kind to me. By working several jobs and living frugally, they had saved some money and were also very generous to us as we set up housekeeping, bought furniture, etc. They were also generous to their grandchildren, giving them most of their money before they died.)

When I think of J.S. as a little boy, two things come to mind: first his energy and secondly his unusual vocabulary. To digress for a moment, I should mention that I was surprised that his Mother and Grandmother never let him cry. The minute he was unhappy, they picked him up. I said they would spoil him, but they didn't know what I was talking about. It was a concept they had never heard of—not a part of the Italian—American vocabulary at all. Then I realized that "spoiling a child" is a metaphor borrowed most likely from fruit that can spoil. The Italian way of raising children differed from that of the Irish, but it worked, and neither of our children could be described as spoiled. End of digression.

Regarding J. S.'s energy, once we took him to his pediatrician for a periodic exam. The nurse placed him on the exam table which was covered with paper. He kicked so hard and so long that he ripped half of the paper off, and she had to lift them up and pull down more paper. As we were leaving she gave him a pin which had on it a picture of an executive with a key in his back and the word "unwind" at the bottom. After he learned to walk, we used to take them to the football field at the College. He loved to run away from us—halfway down the field. When we would call for him to come back, he wouldn't so we'd say "bye, bye" and start to leave. That brought him to us at top speed. One of his favorite games was to take all the pots and pans and cans from the lower kitchen cabinets and spread them around the kitchen floor. His Mother would stand at the sink or stove as he emptied the cabinets. When I came home at noon, I would have to step carefully to get what I needed for lunch. When he took a nap, we put everything away, but after his nap he would take them out again. J.S. had plenty of toys but he preferred to play with pots and pans.

When he began to talk, he had some remarkable neologisms. When he wanted milk, he would point to his cup and say "milkin-in." Doughnuts were "domers" and the basement was the "basem." For "tomorrow" he coined the word "nexterday" by analogy with "yesterday." He called our next-door neighbor Ruben "Rubo" and his first friend Alan was "Honer." He and Allen called me "Waboo" the origin of which was never explained.

We didn't let either of our kids sleep in bed with us, but sometimes before Shannon was born on Saturday morning when we stayed in bed late, we'd let J.S. join us and watch cartoons. One Saturday, when he was probably three or four, he said. "Gee, if Dad died, I could sleep with Mom all the time." Little Oedipus! One day after J.S. learned that Dee was expecting a baby, he started to cry. In reply to our question regarding what was wrong, he said, "If Mom has a baby and people come to the house, they'll all look at the baby instead of me."

I have fewer recollections of Shannon as a baby than I do of J.S. Perhaps this is because she was quieter, less active, and less eccentric. I do remember that not long after she came home from the hospital and used to take naps in a portable crib in the dining room, she would respond to J.S. long before she did to me or even her Mother. He would stand beside the crib, jump up and down, and talk to her and get an immediate reaction, something I couldn't get. Shannon was such a perfect little lady that she never caused any trouble. I can't even recall ever hearing her cry.

One incident does stand out in my mind. Dee and I went somewhere and left the kids with their grandparents who happened to be visiting. While we were gone J.S. misbehaved (he swore at his grandfather). When we returned, Shannon who was in a bouncy chair and couldn't talk yet nevertheless rushed to meet us shouting "Jeje, Jeje," her name for her brother. She had understood what had happened, but didn't have the vocabulary to report it to us. This led me to believe that little kids understand a lot long before they are able to describe anything.

When she learned to talk, she used to say some remarkable things. One day she said to me, "How come when we're in the kitchen, downstairs is the basement, but when we're in the bedroom, downstairs is the kitchen?" I said, "Well, there was a guy named Einstein who dealt with questions like that, and when you grow up, you'll probably understand him better than I do." Years later, when we used to kid her about having so many pairs of shoes and still wanting us to buy more, I told her one day that one of the saints had said, "I felt sorry for myself because I had no shoes and then I met a man who had no feet." She replied immediately, "I felt sorry for myself because my daughter spent all my money on shoes, and then I met a man who didn't have a daughter." The subject of shoes was never mentioned again.

When Shannon was in preschool at Ms. Lyle's School which was near Macalester, she used to sit on a seat over the rear wheel of my bicycle, and I'd take her to and from school. One Halloween she was dressed as Minnie Mouse, and, as I was peddling down Grand Avenue, I suddenly thought, "Here I am riding down one of the main streets in St. Paul with Minnie Mouse on my bike; I hope none of my students see me." I'd pick her up at noon and ride home for lunch. Then I would take a nap as she watched Sesame Street and produced art works. Shannon was always busy coloring, drawing, making things with construction paper and Scotch tape, or sticking stickers on sheets of paper. She was an excellent artist.

In the summer of 1969 we bought our house on Goodrich Avenue was nearly a hundred years old. In the upstairs bathroom there was a door about four feet high that opened into the attic. We had a cleaning lady, a little old lady named Jeanette, who was short to start with but had become bent over with age. Shannon believed that Jeannette lived in the attic and that once a week we let her out to a clean the house.

After her Mother and was diagnosed with cancer, and perhaps after she had passed away, I discovered that Shannon used to stay awake at night writing—filling notebook after notebook with what I believe was a novel. She would not let me read it then and certainly wouldn't let me read it now, and as far as I know no one was ever allowed to see it.

In 1980 we took our first trip with kids visiting the Black Hills of South Dakota. Dee was not expecting much. This may be a hasty generalization, but it is my impression that Italian-Americans don't take the kind of vacations that other Americans take. At least her extended family didn't. Their idea of a vacation was for the whole clan to go to a beach somewhere, for instance Coney Island. They would take their own food, everything but live poultry, as one friend joked, and the women would fix huge evening meals for everybody. Dee's family didn't like to eat out unless it was in an Italian restaurant. They tended not to trust cooks unless they were Italians. This digression is necessary to explain why I had to use all my persuasive powers to persuade her that a road trip to the Black Hills would be fun and would be a good time for the family. Actually we had a wonderful time. We rented a Dodge van that had a table in the back with seats in front and behind it so the kids sat there drawing pictures, coloring, etc. as we drove the 600 or so miles each way. We climbed hills in the Badlands, stopped at the Wall Drug store, stayed at the State Game Lodge where I had worked for a summer after I graduated from high school, saw Mount Rushmore, and all the other sites. Not knowing what the kids would think of Mount Rushmore, before we arrived there, I said to them, "Sometimes you get very excited about something, but when you see it, you're disappointed and quickly tire of it. That's life" J.S. asked, "Do you ever get tired of being a Dad?" I replied, "No, that's different." It was as good a vacation as we ever had. We liked traveling in a van so much, we bought a VW Vanagon upon our return home.

In 1982 we drove our new Vanagon to Knoxville for the World's Fair. From Knoxville we drove through the Blue Ridge Mountains to Richmond, Virginia where one of Shannon's classmates had moved. After visiting her we drove to Washington, D.C. and visited the principal sites there. From D.C. we drove to Jamestown for a weeklong visit, and then the kids, Grandma Santa, and two cousins, Hillary and Elizabeth, returned with us to St. Paul. In 1983 Dee and I took the kids to England and Ireland.

To digress for a moment, a persistent problem during the '70s was what to do during the summers. I took my salary on a nine-month basis so we would have no income during the summer unless I got a research grant or some other type of support. In the summer of 1970 I got a Macalester "Faculty Foreign Fellowship" to participate in a dig at a Roman archaeological site 100 miles south of Paris. Archaeology was something I discussed in many of my classes, but I had never had a course in it, and I felt that it was a gap in my education. That summer Dee and Jerry Sean spent a month or more in Jamestown with her parents.

For three summers I conducted workshops at Macalester for high school teachers of humanities, thanks to a grant from the state of Minnesota. These were highly successful and led to the publication of a little book called *Articulating the Ineffable* which was on teaching interdisciplinary humanities. Even more successful was the establishment of the Macalester Center for the Teaching of Humanities, funded by a National Endowment for the Humanities grant which the chair of the French Department and I won. That took care of us for three more summers. In 1984 and 1986 I took students to Italy through the University of Minnesota's SPAN program which stood for Student Projects for Amity among Nations. This involved meeting with students on Saturdays during the school year and then taking them to Italy for two months during the summer. Each student had a project, for instance "fast food in ancient Rome and modern Italy," "the restoration of artworks," "the importance of soccer in contemporary Italy," etc. During the summer that I was in Italy with SPAN students, Dee and the kids, her Mother and two nieces, Hillary and Elizabeth, came for a couple of weeks, and after showing them the sites of Rome, I drove them down south to Calabria so that Santa could visit the city that her parents lived in before they came to the United States. This trip and the trip to Ireland enabled the kids to visit the lands from which their ancestors had come.

In 1985 I recruited a group of twenty-five Latin teachers and graduate students of Classics to study in Rome with Fr. Foster, one of the Pope's Latin secretary. (details later)

In January of 1987 when J.S. was nineteen and Shannon thirteen, Dee began having back problems. One of her doctors had her doing exercises on the living room floor. Eventually she found the right doctor and was diagnosed with metastatic breast cancer. This was a terrible shock to the whole family. Dee had always watched her diet, had exercised, and came from a family that enjoyed longevity. In addition after she began teaching at St. Catherines, she taught a course called "wellness" which dealt with how to stay healthy.

Dee had a wonderful doctor named Dr. Crandall; no one ever had a better doctor. When she told him she wanted to be around when Shannon graduated from high school in four years, he told her to aim for two years, celebrate, and then aim for two more years. She lived twenty-two months. Dealing with her sickness and death could be the subject of a whole book, but suffice it to say here that I believe she was disturbed by prednisone part of the time. But she had plenty to be upset and angry about. Each time we came to a fork in the road when she could have received good news or bad news, the news was bad. She passed away peacefully on November 2, 1988 with her Mother, J.S., Shannon and me at the bedside. Her last words were, "Don't worry about me. I'm going to be okay." Obviously her faith gave her strength and consolation at the last moment. No children ever had a better Mother, nor did any children ever love their Mother more, and no Mother ever loved her children more. Losing their Mother was a tragedy of immeasurable dimensions, but they not only survived, they have flourished, buoyed up, I believe, by their faith and their memories of her and of a happy childhood.

Much to my surprise and delight both of my kids decided to go into medicine. I fear that I cannot take much credit for this. Most likely they were influenced by their Mother, but as kids they had also observed the lifestyle (a word I hate and usually avoid) of their uncle, the oral surgeon and a cousin in Jamestown who was a surgeon. Both J.S. and Shannon won early admission to the University of Minnesota Medical School while still at St. Thomas. J.S. is a pulmonologist, and Shannon a pediatrician. J.S. married Brenda Tegelman on June 6, 1998. They have two girls, Carissa born on January 4, 2000 and Briana born on October 23, 2002. Shannon married Mike Parkos, a police officer, on June 24, 2005. On May 17, 2008 (my birthday) she gave birth to twins, Josie and John.

About five years after Dee passed away mutual friends introduced me to Mary Ann Roel, a native of North Dakota. After a divorce from her first husband, Mary Ann had gone back to college, earned a degree, and moved to Minneapolis where she has relatives and worked for the legal department of a corporation negotiating contracts with attorneys. Mary Ann is a many splendored person. I shall attempt to describe some of these splendors under the following headings: Mary Ann the artist, the animal lover, the collector, the traveler, and the mother. The first thing that struck me about Mary Ann was her beauty. Although she is only three years younger than I am, every now and then to this day total strangers will come up to us and compliment her on her beautiful features. This external beauty is matched by an inner beauty, and it is only a slight exaggeration to say that Mary Ann lives for beauty. She has a great appreciation for natural beauty, especially flowers, trees, mountains, and even the desert. Being an artist she also produces beauty. She was well known for her watercolors in North Dakota where she belonged to a local gallery, had numerous shows, and won many awards. Mary Ann also does ink drawings, etchings, acrylics, and even an occasional stone sculpture. At one time she took up welding, but chose not to pursue that approach to art.

Before moving to Minneapolis she taught watercolors for the public schools and conducted workshops for other artists. Her first husband was a contractor, and she decorated the houses he built. Our townhouse is proof of her talent as an interior decorator. The flowers at the entrance to our townhouse rival those of anyone else in the development. (She also raises beautiful tomatoes.) Photography is another passion, and we have a wonderful collection of photos taken on all our various trips, some of which appear in this volume.

Among her many other passions, animals have played an important role in her life. Until her horse, Scarlet, died last fall at age 27 (Mary Ann owned her for 25 years), she had always had at least one horse and often more. Mary Ann also raised and showed smooth, standard dachshunds. Her dog, John, was an American and Canadian champion. (She also showed Siamese cats and quarter horses.) Mary Ann has an encyclopedic knowledge of animal behavior, not only of horses and dogs, but of many other animals too. I have often told her she should have gone into ethology, the study of animal behavior.

An accomplishment she is rightfully proud of is having been one of three persons who opened an office for the Fargo-Moorhead Humane Society. Related to that enterprise was her practice of nursing injured animals and birds back to health at home, including on one occasion a fully grown pelican. She appeared on television several times a week as a spokesperson for the Humane Society, urging listeners to adopt animals.

It is difficult to know where to start describing Mary Ann, the collector. She collects rocks (small, large, and very large). Many of the latter which include huge pieces of petrified wood, I had not noticed until we moved five years ago. She also has a great love for gems and jewelry. Getting Mary Ann to walk past a jewelry store is more difficult than steering an alcoholic past a bar. She has been able to indulge her love of gems and all things lapidary in Tucson which annually hosts the largest rock and gem show in the world. Combining her interest in rocks, gems, and glass with her love of animals has resulted in a frog collection which includes examples from ¼ inch to monsters a foot high. Mary Ann also has an impressive collection of Indian artifacts (arrow heads, an anchor, hammer stones and other tools), shells, and pre-Columbian art objects.

Before we met, Mary Ann had traveled extensively in Mexico, South America, Portugal, and Spain. She is a good traveler in the sense that she is prompt and well organized. She has often been more intrepid than I am, wanting to see one more cathedral, one more museum, or one more monument long after I've expressed an interest in "calling it a day." Traveling is an art, and thanks to Mary Ann's help, we have never experienced any of the nightmares that can occur to travelers such as losing a passport, wandering into the wrong part of a town and getting mugged, missing a train or boat, spending the day sitting of a curb somewhere, falling victim to a con artist, etc. Finally, Mary Ann is an avid skier and even managed to persuade me to take it up at age sixty!

Mary Ann has three sons (Jeff, David and Mike) and four grandchildren: Mandy, Kevin, Bethany, and Ben.

Shannon, Dee, and Jerry Sean ca. 1982

In Saint Peter's Square, 1984. From left, Jerry Sean, Cousins Hillary and
Elizabeth, Shannon, Jerry Sr. Not visible Dee and Santa.

Mary Ann and Jerry on Wedding Day, January 6, 1994

With Beloved 1968 MG

Brenda, Briana, Carissa, and Jerry Sean

Mike and Shannon with twins John and Josie

CHAPTER XI

REFORMING EDUCATION: K-12 AND HIGHER

Education is not the filling of a pail
but the lighting of a fire.
W.B. Yeats

Something new is always better
even if it's not as good.
Irish proverb

NAS and MAS

The National Association of Scholars grew out of an organization called the Campus Coalition for Democracy which was founded in the early 1980s by a group of largely Jewish scholars in New York City. They were dismayed by trends that were emerging in higher education such as anti-Americanism, anti-Western bias, and the lowering of academic standards. In 1986 they decided to change their name to the National Association of Scholars (NAS) and go national. In time there were chapters in 49 states with about 6000 members. Eventually too there were spinoff organizations such as the Association of Literary Scholars and Critics, the History Society, and assorted allied organizations such as the Foundation for Individual Rights in Education and the American Council for Trustees and Alumni. The members of these organizations were traditionalists, as far as education was concerned, but both liberal and conservative, as far as politics were concerned. Our opponents in the culture war liked to call us right wing reactionaries.

Around a 1986 I was informed that Stephen Balch, one of the founders of NAS, was coming to Carleton College to meet with professors who were also concerned about recent developments in higher education. Kathy

Kirsten, who later gained fame or perhaps I should say in notoriety, as a columnist for the Minneapolis Star Tribune and I attended the meeting. It was an event that changed the course of my career and my life. Professor Balch urged us to form a chapter of NAS which we did. It was called the Minnesota Association of Scholars and during our peak years we had 140 members. I was elected the first president of our state organization and also a member of the national board of directors. A memorable part of the early MAS years were weekly luncheons at the University of Minnesota Faculty Club which were attended by some very distinguished U of M faculty members., It was an honor for me, a humble professor from a liberal arts college, to participate in these discussions. Many of the trends we discussed were in their infancy and were exceedingly shocking at the time although as time passed they became commonplace. An egregious episode which attracted national attention was the charging of the whole Department of Scandinavian Studies with the creation of an environment hostile to women. Complaints ranged from "professor so-and-so failed to greet me in a friendly manner as we passed in the hall" to charges of sexism in lectures.

Another development that attracted national attention was the "takeover" from our standpoint of the Humanities Program by radicals. The program had been essentially a great books curriculum divided into courses such as "The Periclean Age," the "Augustine Age," the "Middle Ages," etc. up to the modern world. When radical left wing profs became the majority in the program, they voted to abolish all of these courses and replace them with what students called "Marxist indoctrination courses" which was an accurate description. The gutting of the humanities curriculum at the U. of M. attracted national attention thanks mostly to actions taken by NAS member Lynne Cheney. Mrs. Cheney was then head of the National Endowment for the Humanities, and she repeatedly referred to what had happened in Minnesota to the humanities program. During the early years of MAS I put out a newsletter, and we held an annual banquet at which distinguished visitors such as Mrs. Cheney herself spoke.

Around 2000 it was suggested by the Board of NAS that Minnesota and Wisconsin share a full-time executive director who would move back and forth between the Twin Cities and Madison. NAS agreed to pay his salary the first year during which he was to raise funds for various activities and for his salary for future years. Unfortunately this did not work out as will be explained below.

In 2002 Norman Fruman, the second president of MAS, and I were honored in Washington DC by NAS. As a part of the ceremony each of us was allotted at a few minutes to respond. It was an important event in my life and was attended by such well-known scholars and thinkers as Judge Bork, Michael Novak, Irving Kristol, his wife Gertrude Himmelfarb and other academic celebrities. Following is the text of my talk:

I joined the faculty of Macalester College in the fall of 1968. Much to my surprise, I discovered at the first faculty meeting that I could not understand what my new colleagues were talking about. They were using words such as commitment, worldview and values and phrases such as value judgments and values clarification. There was talk of life-styles and of finding a life-style. Liberal arts education was defined by a member of the Psychology Department as "self-actualizing." I would have understood them better if they had been speaking Greek. It was a while before I figured out that, while I was studying in Italy and then leading a rather sheltered life in the Classics Department at the University of Michigan, the Academy had adopted a new way of talking. Academicians had found what Richard Rorty calls "a more attractive vocabulary." But it wasn't until 1987 when Allan Bloom's book *The Closing of the American Mind* appeared, that I understood fully what had happened. Bloom explained that reason had been replaced by commitment; virtues had been replaced by values; the soul had been replaced by the self; true and false had been replaced by authentic and inauthentic; God had been replaced by the sacred; the search for the Good had been replaced by choosing a life-style; and the notion of the common good hadn't been replaced by anything—it was simply abandoned. Talk about communication had become very common; this was because people had given up trying to understand each other; they were just trying to communicate.

All of this is explained brilliantly by Bloom, especially in the chapter entitled "The Nietzscheanization of the Left or Vice Versa." My colleagues were speaking the language of values relativism; never mind that our way of life was founded on absolutes. It was "nihilism American style," or "nihilism with a happy ending," as Bloom dubbed it. Our new president, Arthur Fleming, explained in his inaugural address that "the pursuit of excellence" was an out-moded slogan that had been replaced by the "individualization of learning." That became in the vernacular "doing your own thing." (Come to think of it "doing your own thing" may have replaced the notion of sacrificing for the common good.) The few times I screwed up my courage to enter debates at faculty meetings, I discovered that my colleagues couldn't understand me either. After a while, that didn't really matter since most of them had stopped talking to me anyway. For many years I literally had no one to talk to about subjects that mattered most to me such as the philosophy of education. Let me give you a couple of examples which will illustrate the sad state of affairs.

In 1975 forty-five of our seniors, who were about to graduate, were interviewed by a team of faculty members from the Associated Colleges of the Midwest. Among other things our students were asked to define or describe a liberal arts education. Several said, "If this is a liberal arts college, I must have a liberal arts education." One said that a liberal arts college is a small college. A couple said that a liberal arts college is one that attracts liberals. Most said that the word *liberal* in the phrase *liberal arts education* means you are "free to do your own thing." The visitors observed that these students had apparently never been involved in a discussion of liberal arts education before, nor had they ever given the subject any thought. If forty-five members of our faculty had been interviewed, the answers would not have been any better.

A colleague from the English Department once told me that there was no longer a consensus about the liberal arts so we were free to do whatever we wanted to and free to call anything we wanted a liberal arts education. The students weren't the only ones doing their own thing! I used to say that there was only one thing all my colleagues agreed upon, namely that "critical thinking" was one of the goals of liberal arts education. Then a few years ago I discovered that by "critical thinking" some of my younger colleagues meant "being critical of Western Civilization."

I once wrote an essay for the faculty newsletter discussing the invention of liberal arts education by the sophists, and its development by Plato, Aristotle, Cicero, Quintilian, and others, tracing its history through the Middle Ages to the Renaissance. I also argued that we needed a core curriculum. I was labeled an essentialist and told that my colleagues, who were existentialists when it came to education, considered essentialism not only unenlightened but very wicked. Educational existentialists held, and perhaps still hold, that liberal arts education cannot be defined. Rather students go to a liberal arts college for four years, and then after graduation they look back and say "Ah that was a liberal arts education!"

From 1960, when I first taught Latin as a teaching fellow, the field of classics has been under attack. At first it was the professors of education. Then during the late 60s the students claimed the classics weren't relevant. A decade or so after that we began being accused of racism, sexism, classism, ethnocentrism, et cetera because all the works we were teaching were written by DWEMS. Three times at Macalester during periods of financial exigency our department was threatened with abolition. I spent most of my time justifying what we were doing and defending, first the study of Latin and Greek, then of the classics themselves, then of the humanities, then of the liberal arts, then of Western civilization. Note that the scope gets broader and broader. If I live long enough I would not be surprised to find myself on a space ship defending Earth Studies or even Galactic studies before a crew of little green men.

Now, constantly having to justify one's self could get a person down. Eventually, I decided to make a virtue out of necessity. I began to think of myself as a controversialist and polemicist. I wrote essays for the faculty newsletter and the school paper plus an occasional op-ed piece for the local newspaper. I followed Jerry Graff's advice to Teach The Conflicts, offering a January term course titled one year "Bennet, Bloom and Hirsch" and other years "Contemporary Controversies," in which we read and discussed such books as *Tenured Radicals, The Closing of the American Mind, Cultural Literacy* and so forth. Conservative students who took the course reveled in the opportunity to express their true opinions for a change.

Then about fourteen years ago something happened that saved my career and perhaps my sanity. Out of the blue I received an invitation to attend a meeting in Northfield at the home of two Carleton College professors, and there we were introduced to one Steve Balch. Steve described a new organization he and others were founding to be called the National Association of Scholars. Suddenly I learned that there were others as concerned as I was about what was happening to American higher education. I discovered that right there in Minnesota there were people I could talk to, people who shared my rather traditional philosophy of education. The rest is history, as the saying goes. I shall always be grateful to Steve, to Herb London, Nelson Ong, Peter Shaw and Barry Gross of happy memory, and others such as Irving Kristol who got the Campus Coalition for Democracy, from which NAS evolved, up and going. And it is an honor to receive an award named for Barry Gross; I am very grateful indeed.

When I began teaching there were certain words we weren't supposed to say in the presence of girls; now there is only one word we're not supposed to say in their presence: "girls." I want, however, to end on a happy note and say in closing that in spite of everything I have had a wonderful career. When I meet people and discover that they think teaching dead languages must be dull and boring, I tell them, on the contrary, that if my career had been any more exciting, I could not have stood it.

A year ago the *Chronicle of Higher Education* did a story on our department as one of the most flourishing Classics Departments in the country. We have thirty majors; all of our non-language courses are full each semester, and we have very good enrollments in the three classical languages we offer, Latin, Greek and Hebrew. Our average class size is right up there with economics and biology. Our graduates are studying at Oxford, Princeton, Berkeley, the University of Michigan, and so forth. Besides charismatic teachers, it is archeology that is attracting the students, but they return each fall from excavating in Israel motivated to study classical languages, literature, and history. A Spanish proverb comes to mind: "Living well is the best revenge."

According to the author of a book on postmodernism, the postmodern period began in the U. S. at 3:32 p.m. on 15 July 1972 when the Pruitt-Igoe housing development in St. Louis, Missouri, came crashing down. It may be that the postmodern era ended at 9:59 a.m. on the morning of 11 September 2001 when the South Tower of the World Trade Center came crashing down. If so, at least one good thing has come from that tragedy.

As indicated in Chapter VIII and in my NAS talk above I was very unhappy with the changes that were made Macalister in the late 1960s and early '70s, for example the elimination of required courses such as freshman English and foreign languages. But this was only the beginning of the destruction of the liberal arts curriculum and liberal arts education as it had been known since the time of the Sophists in the fifth century B.C. Here from an NAS brochure is a list of what concerned NAS and MAS:

> Decline of academic standards, politicization of scholarship and teaching, the substitution of social reform for the pursuit of knowledge, use of sexual, racial or other criteria unrelated to merit in hiring, in promotion and in student recruitment, denigration of great literary and artistic works, inappropriate use of sexual, racial and other non-scholarly criteria in selecting works to be studied, dogmatic hostility to Western civilization, turning the study of non-Western cultures into an instrument for denouncing American society, unscholarly curricular innovation which often supplant substantive and intellectually challenging courses, absence of core curricula or other requirements ensuring a

well-rounded education, unfair treatment of colleagues suspected of holding 'politically incorrect views,' use of non-curricular resources such as orientations and residential life programs to impose political and ideological conformity, decline in civility on college and university campuses, suppression of students' freedoms of speech and association, tendency of administrators to placate activists rather than enforce rules even-handedly, racial polarization on campuses, policies promoting polarization, deleterious influence of low standards in higher education on the quality of education in the lower schools, and inadequate preparation of high school graduates for college work.

For NAS the two paramount issues were racial preferences and radical feminist theory. MAS members were most passionate about freedom of expression for students who held unorthodox views and were therefore often silenced.

The MAS had its ups and downs and was losing members because most were senior faculty and, as they retired, we could not recruit new members fast enough to replace them. In addition sharing an executive director with Wisconsin hadn't worked out chiefly because he was unable to get along with the members of the Wisconsin chapter and because he was unable to raise enough money to pay his salary in Minnesota. When he resigned about the same time as I was retiring, I volunteered to be the executive director. As I was looking through the files for recent years, I notice that Stanley Hubbard, a local billionaire and owner of radio and TV stations, had given us small amounts of money each year for several years. I wrote Mr. Hubbard and a told him of our efforts to revitalize the organization, and I asked him if he could help us bring David Horowitz to St. Paul to speak at our annual banquet. Fortunately for us Mr. Hubbard was a great admirer of David Horowitz, and he offered to give Horvitz a $6000 honorarium and pay all of his travel and hospitality expenses. That spring we had over a hundred at our banquet whereas the previous four or five years we had been lucky to get to twenty. At the time Horowitz was promoting his Academic Bill of Rights, trying to get legislators to adopt it so that students who were to the right of center would have their right to freedom of expression speech guaranteed. Horowitz delivered a fiery speech full of dreadful examples of students whose grades had been negatively affected because of their conservative views and so forth.

After the talk Bruce Hendry, a local philanthropist and head of the Hendry Family Foundation, told me that he would like to make a substantial donation to support our work. He said to send him a proposal before the end of the year. Meanwhile Jim van Houten, a retired CEO of an insurance company, who taught at the Carlson School of Management, had been elected president of MAS. I drafted a proposal that asked for $10,000 or so, and sent it to Jim. He reworked it and raised the amount to $49,000. I assumed that Bruce would laugh when he saw the amount. Instead here's what he said, "I'll give you $25,000, and if you can match that, I'll give you another $25,000 to start an endowment." Clearly I had not been thinking big enough. Jim and I went to work to raise $25,000. The first person I called was Mr. Hubbard's Secretary. I asked if she thought he might have half an hour sometime soon when Jim and I could stop in and talk to him, and I outlined briefly our plan to found a center at the University of Minnesota. A few minutes later the telephone rang and a voice said "Hi, it's Stan Hubbard. I hear you want to bring some right wing nuts to the University to counterbalance all the left-wing nuts they've got over there." I was speechless for a moment or two. It was the first time I had ever talked to a billionaire. When I regained my composure I said, "Yes, that's essentially what we're trying to do." Mr. Hubbard then said, "I'm having breakfast tomorrow morning with a number of friends who might be interested too. Send me a proposal and I'll talk to them." I emailed a proposal to him and a few days later the checks started coming in the mail. Hubbard himself sent $5000 as did several of his friends. Other checks for $3000 and $2000 showed up in my mailbox plus one for $1000 from Wyoming. "This" I thought, "is a way to raise money—have the philanthropists themselves do the fund-raising for you." Meanwhile Jim who had lots of wealthy friends had also been on the phone, and his friends sent us checks as did our own members. By December 31 we had raised $40,000, more than enough for Bruce Hendry to give us the extra $25,000. Hence in less than a month MAS's bank account went from about $1200 to over $90,000.

I used to quote a favorite verse from the Bible, specifically from the Book of Proverbs: "A feast is made for laughter and wine maketh merry, but money answer of all things." With money there were many things we could do. We persuaded Ian Maitland who taught at the Carlson School of Management and had run for Congress a couple times to be the head of our proposed center. He suggested calling it "The Toqueville Center for the Study of Free Institutions," and he wrote an excellent mission statement. Almost immediately we were sponsoring lectures by nationally known speakers and scholars such as Ward Connerly who spoke against racial preferences in higher education, Victor Davis Hanson, a very distinguished classicist an war historian whose talk was entitled "Why We Must Stay the Course in Iraq." Other speakers included Alan Kors, one of the founders of FIRE, the Foundation for Individual Rights in Education, and Ahmed Samatar of Macalister College who discussed problems plaguing certain Islamic countries. Our own members also gave talks. My talk was cosponsored by the School of Education and was entitled "The Failure of Progressive Education and the Return to Classical Models." It was well attended and was not exactly what the professors of education were expecting. I gave a slightly edited version of the paper I had delivered the previous summer in Greece. It was a diatribe against John Dewey and his philosophy of education and constituted for me something I had wanted to do for many years. In spite of the polemical nature of what I said the discussion was rational and constructive. In essence I blamed the schools of education for most of the serious problems of the public school system.

In one respect we failed with the Tocqueville Center since we never succeeded in getting it recognized as an official University of Minnesota Institute. The U has about one hundred centers and institutes of various types. Type one receives no funds from the University. Type two can receive up to $50,000 per year and is given space for a secretary. Type three is eligible to receive up to $100,000 per year and has cross-listed courses. The highest type, such as the Cancer Institute, receives millions of dollars each year from grants from the government and from the University and has its own faculty members. Our humble center was Ian Maitland's office, and we receive no university funds. We had been led to believe that a university professor could simply declare himself a center, notify the dean of the action and *ipso facto* the center would exist. We found the process not that easy. Administrator after administrator found reasons not to approve our proposal—a center such as the Tocqueville Center didn't belong in the Business School—they were revising the approval process—the Dean had resigned and the acting Dean didn't want to approve any new centers, etc. As of this writing Toqueville operates without university approval, but this has not prevented us from sponsoring exciting and valuable programs that bring "intellectual diversity" to the University community.

Improving the Teaching of Latin

Around 1974 I read in the *Classical Journal* that a new institute had been founded in Rome called *Institutum Altioris Latinitatis* in which classes would be conducted in Latin, all textbooks would be in Latin, and likewise all exams, both written and oral. Since this is the way philosophy and theology were taught at the Gregorian University when I studied there from 1956 to 1958, I knew it was the best, and perhaps for most people, the only way to really learn the language. Hence I wrote a letter to the rector of the new institute asking him if he would be interested in having me recruit a group of graduate students and Latin teachers to come to Rome for a month or so of "total immersion" in Latin.

Ten years passed and I hadn't heard from him, and I had more or less forgotten about the project. Then one day in 1984 I received a letter from a certain Fr. Foster who said he had been visiting the rector at the *Institutum Altioris Latinitatis,* and my letter was lying on his desk! (I assumed it had been lying there for ten years, but a friend who was familiar with the Italian postal service reminded me that it might have just been delivered!) Fr. Foster said that he would be interested in teaching a course such as the one I had proposed if I would recruit the students. A little research revealed that Fr. Reginald Foster was an American friar and member of the Discalced Carmelites from Milwaukee who worked in the Vatican in the Secretariat of State translating documents into Latin. Since I was planning to be in Rome in the summer of 1984 with a group of students (and also with my family), I arranged to meet with Fr. Foster and discuss the particulars.

We had our discussion in Rome that summer, and it appeared that we agreed on everything. I would advertise the course in classical journals and through a mailing to Latin teachers; it would be a Macalester College summer session course; students would pay tuition to Macalester; Fr. Foster and I would each receive one month' salary, and the course would be team-taught. I sent letters to 1,000 Latin teachers, and put ads in journals. Around twenty-five participants signed up, paid their tuition, and showed up in Rome. From that point on nothing went as I had planned. First of all Fr. Foster refused to accept any money, and he didn't like the fact that the students had paid tuition. Secondly, it was obvious from the first moment of the first class that this would be a one-man show. Hence I sat in the class with the students, and he treated me as a student which didn't bother me since I was learning a lot.

To explain Fr. Foster's teaching methods, I have often referred to Professor Rassias of Dartmouth College who became internationally known for his innovative approach to teaching French. (Anyone who is interested should "google" his name and learn about his work and the Foundation that is now named after him.) Professor Rassias used to go to class dressed as Louis XIV or Moliere or some other French character. He would throw chairs, kiss girls, tear his clothes, and do other outrageous things all the while speaking French. Before the students realized it, they were drawn in and were speaking French. As with Professor Rassias, each of Fr. Foster's classes was a "happening" although he didn't kiss the girls or tear his clothes. It was "wild" as the students put it, and one never knew what might happen. First of all everything was in Latin which is not easy to do. Secondly, he would, for instance, open *Time Magazine*, point to an advertisement, and call on someone to translate into Latin "Pan Am flies to more countries than any other airline." There were no textbooks. He would rise early each morning (around 4:00) and make out worksheets. The passages came from all periods of Latin—early inscriptions, classical Latin, Latin of the Silver Age, church fathers, medieval Latin, Renaissance Latin, and finally modern Latin, e.g. documents such as papal encyclicals that he had worked on or was working on. The sessions lasted from around 2:00 p.m. until 5:00. For those who wanted more Latin he began having evening sessions under the trees (*sub arboribus*).

On weekends there were excursions, e.g. we went to Pompeii where we read graffiti. After visiting the site everyone was exhausted since it was a very hot day, but, since Fr. Foster knew one of the guards at nearby Herculaneum who would let us into areas that were not yet open to the public, we had to go there. Students who were half his age could barely keep up with him; he seemed to be preternaturally energetic. Another weekend he took us on his "obelisk tour" which later became famous. He led us from piazza to piazza in Rome requiring us to translate all the Latin inscriptions, and they are very numerous. We got a tour of the Roman Forum which was totally in Latin. A crowd gathered around listening, but I'm not sure they realized that Latin was being spoken again in the Forum. There were also excursions out into the countryside, e.g. to Horace's farm, Cicero's birthplace, and Castel Gandolfo, the Pope's summer residence, where we sang "My Darling Clementine" in Latin and the cows gathered around us. (No papal bulls, however.)

The program was a huge success, and he has continued it each summer through 2008, taking 2009 off because of poor health. From the small beginning in 1985 it grew into a world-famous program consisting of three 90-minute sessions running from 2:00 p.m. until 6:30, the first session is for the *juniores*, the second session is a joint session, and the third one is for the *seniores*. Fr. Foster is without doubt now the most famous Latin teacher in the world. He has been written up in numerous scholarly and popular journals; there have been TV specials, and he has conducted workshops in the U.S. When Mary Ann and I visited his class a few years ago, he hailed me as the founder of the program, but as I said above, it was a one-man show from the first minute of the first class. The fact that I was not involved after the first summer doesn't really bother me. A very large number of Latin scholars and teachers are better at what they do because of Fr. Foster's program.

Reforming K-12 Education

In 1996 Mike Ritchie whom I had met at various meetings of people dedicated to reforming the public schools asked me if I would be interested in joining him in an effort to found a charter school. Charter schools are public schools, and they receive public funds, but they are independent, that is they are not run by a school district. Instead each charter school has a sponsor and is run by a school board consisting of teachers, parents, and community members. Not being under a school district is supposed to foster innovation and eliminate red tape. Charter schools are typically started by groups of parents and or teachers and individuals who are dissatisfied with traditional public education. The charter school movement began in Minnesota and spread to the rest of the nation. There are many very successful charter schools, but of course there have been some notable failures too, as is to be expected. Mike was an educational reformer *par excellence,* but his degree and his experience were in administration and business. I believe he was looking for someone with academic credentials to work with him. I immediately expressed my willingness to join him in this venture, but on one condition—the school would have to be a Core Knowledge school. I don't think Mike had heard of Core Knowledge so I loaned him E.D. Hirsch's book *Cultural Literacy.* After reading it he called me and said, "This is exactly the kind of curriculum we want."

In order to explain what is unique about Core Knowledge I must review the work of E.D. Hirsch whom I consider one of the greatest educational reformers in the history of the West. It is a pleasure for me to do this and I never miss an opportunity to spread the message. Few things are as important as the philosophy of education.

I summarize the main points made by Hirsch as follows: 1) Communication among citizens is essential if democracy is to work and if citizens are to participate intelligently in democratic processes. 2) Intelligent communication is impossible without literacy. Every American should be able to read newspapers and serious books that are addressed to the general public. 3) Evidence from many quarters points to a serious decline in "communication skills" among young people in recent decades. 4) We cannot blame TV, the breakdown of the family, poverty, racism, or underfunding of schools for this decline. 5) The "chief cause of our educational failures in the domain of literacy" is a misguided philosophy of education based on the romantic notion that each child has an "inborn, instinctive tendency to follow its own proper development." For this reason the content of education is arbitrary; any interesting content will do as long as the student is developing the desired skills such as problem-solving, decision making, critical thinking, analysis and synthesis. So-called "progressive" schools are based on this philosophy, as is the *laissez-faire,* "do your own thing," design-your-own-curriculum approach to education that has flourished in many colleges and universities since the 1960's.

Hirsch called the idea that the content of education is arbitrary "educational formalism," and he made a convincing case for the proposition that defining the goals of education in terms of skills without teaching a specific body of knowledge is a mistake which has had devastating effects, especially on the ability to read. Reading, which is the basic skill, is not a general skill that can be developed in the abstract or *in vacuo.* Being able to read differs from text to text and requires "specific background knowledge" which writers assume readers have. (Reading *The New England Journal of Medicine* is one thing; reading a Harry Potter book another.) Writers in our culture do not identify Jesus or Plato but should identify, for example, Jacques Derrida when writing for the general public. Jesus and Plato are part of the background knowledge writers expect readers to have; Derrida isn't. Schools that want their graduates to be literate should teach the shared background knowledge that literate people in our culture (i.e., those who are able to read and write) possess. This is the inherited body of knowledge on which the culture is based, and transmitting it to the younger generation has been the purpose of education in all cultures, ancient and modern, with the possible exception of our own since the 1960's.

What readers need to know in order to read with ease, enjoyment, and understanding is an empirical question which can be answered empirically, and this is what Hirsch and his associates did. Assuming that high school graduates should be able to read newspapers, magazines such as *Time* and *Newsweek,* and books addressed to the general public, Hirsch and his associates went through publications of this sort asking in each case, "What did the writers assume that the readers knew?" or, put in another way, "What historical figures, authors, events, allusions, foreign phrases, scientific concepts, etc. did the writers not explain?" The result was a list of 5,000 items which was subsequently printed in a sixty-three page appendix to *Cultural Literacy.* He thus identified the contents of high school-level cultural literacy, and this list constitutes the basis of the enormously successful Core Knowledge curriculum.

I readily admit that Mike did the lion's share of the work in starting our school which was and is known as the New Spirit School. Our idea was to start a school which would give a certain number of students a superior education, one might say an education such as students get in elite private schools where parents pay thousands of dollars per year in tuition. But, of course, they would pay no tuition at our school. Mike had studied and read about public education for five years, and in addition he had connections in the State Department of Education and elsewhere which helped us tremendously. He filed the forms, and located two former Catholic schools for us to use. I was chair of the founding committee and of the school board after the school opened in 1998. Mike used to say one of my most important jobs was to provide a shoulder for him to cry on. The school is located in Frogtown, a low income neighborhood in St. Paul. Much to our surprise the first year 75% of our students were Hmong. Many Hmong people, we learned, did not like the large traditional public schools and felt that their children were neglected there. A small local school was exactly what they wanted. Since many of the kindergartners and first-graders didn't speak English, we had to hire special teachers and interpreters and a Hmong parent coordinator. Thanks to the fact that Mike was an excellent administrator, everything worked out and the New Spirit School was and is a huge success

There was, however, one incident which I should mention since it illustrates the unexpected sort of thing that can happen. Mike hired a member of the Hmong community to help recruit students. He was given a contract that stated clearly that this was a temporary position which would last a specific number of months. This gentleman was a prominent member of the community who was well-educated, spoke French and English well and in addition had a regular program on their radio station. Somehow he became convinced that his position was a continuing one and that he was in line to become the assistant director of the school or play some other important role there. When Mike informed him that this was not the case and that in fact his term was up (he had not incidentally recruited many students) he became exceedingly angry. During the Christmas break he called Hmong parents and told them that the school was closing and that they should transfer their children to another school. He also told him that we were racists, that we were treating their children "worse than dogs," that there had been cases of food poisoning and other lies. Perhaps most damaging of all he told them that the building was haunted. (We were told that many Hmong believed in ghosts and were very superstitious.) As a result of this we lost approximately 100 students in the middle of the school year, and this gentleman nearly succeeded in destroying the school. Fortunately Mike was able to lease one of our two buildings, and we consolidated the remaining students in one building. This saved the school. The following fall many of the students who had transferred drifted back, and our enrollment rose again to an acceptable level. (Enrollment was and is vital since we receive so much per student from the state.) As far as our nemesis was concerned, we assumed that he had spread the word that he was going to have an important position in the administration of the school, and when that didn't happen, he lost face which caused his anger.

When I retired in the spring of 2003 I was asked myself over and over, "What can I do now to serve society and my fellow human beings?" I planned to continue reading, doing research, and writing, but I wanted to do more than that. Finally I decided to try starting another Core Knowledge charter school. I should explain that my enthusiasm for Core Knowledge is matched only by my antipathy and even hatred of so-called progressive education. My conviction that progressive education is a philosophy of education that is totally mistaken and is the cause of many, if not most, of the problems of the traditional public schools dates backs to 1953 or 1954 when I took an education course at the University of South Dakota. I confess too that I was influenced by Grace Beede, my mentor, who also had a very low opinion of progressive education. Progressive educators from John Dewey on have always opposed the study of Latin and Greek and the classics and have done what they could to banish these subjects from both K-12 schools and institutions of higher learning. In 2007 I delivered a paper at an international conference on education in Greece entitled "The Failure of Progressive Education and the Return to Classical Models." In this paper I discussed what I consider the nineteen most serious errors committed by progressive educators and why we should return to the philosophy of education and understanding of human nature that is based on Plato, Aristotle, and the Biblical tradition. That paper can be found in my book *More in Love with Logos*.

Returning now to my retirement in 2003, I decided to try starting another Core Knowledge charter school. I quickly learned that the situation had changed drastically and for the better since Mike and I began planning the New Spirit School in 1996. For one thing companies had sprung up to help founders of charter schools. I knew a couple of people who worked for a company called School Start so I decided to seek their help. They, especially Johana Sand, worked with us step-by-step until the school opened. By us I mean the founding committee I put together. It consisted of three classicists, a lawyer, and a certified teacher. The best thing School Start did was write the proposals which brought us both state and federal funds for which they received a percentage. The process went smoothly except for two glitches one minor and one major. First School Start went bankrupt, but it was not a huge problem since we had our funding, and Ms. Sand began working for us full-time as our "professional start up coordinator." The major glitch came at the 11th hour—we were unable to find a suitable building in Richfield, the suburb in which we were planning to locate the school. We had visited empty warehouses, former Catholic schools, empty office buildings, theaters, etc. but nothing was quite right. When it appeared that we would have to postpone the opening for a year, Ms Sand and her assistant made approximately 200 telephone calls and finally located a church in Bloomington, one suburb south of Richfield, which had purchased a former public school and had many rooms that were only used on Wednesday evenings and Sunday mornings. This building turned out to be perfect for us so we worked out a lease agreement with the church, and we were in business. No major alterations were required, and the only stumbling block was one long hall that had Biblical scenes painted on it. The State Department of Education said that they had to be covered up or painted over since a public school cannot display religious scenes, statues, symbols or anything of that sort. The pastors of the church resisted but eventually saw that there was no choice.

The second big break also came at the eleventh hour—we got our first choice to be the director of the school. This was Margaret O'Brien who had majored in accounting at Marquette University, graduated from law school, and practiced law for fifteen years, and then left law to become a teacher because she felt she was not contributing enough to society as a lawyer. She then became the principal of a Core Knowledge school in Chicago. For personal reasons she wanted to relocate, and we were very fortunate to get her. Margaret is an exceedingly energetic, even charismatic, administrator and a very talented leader. Ms Sand supervised the recruiting of students sending out 80,000 flyers announcing the opening of school. We hoped to recruit 140 students for two sections of kindergarten and one of first grade, second grade, and one of third grade. Instead we got 254 confirmed registrations which allowed us to add a third section of kindergarten and one of fourth and fifth grade. What we had begun calling the Richfield Classical Academy became the Seven Hills Classical Academy. Seven Hills suggests Rome and also the seven liberal arts. Today it is a flourishing school, and I see no reason why it will not continue flourishing for many years to come. Ms. O'Brien quickly gave the school a distinctive personality and culture centering around the eagle which the students chose as their symbol. The Seven Hills Classical Academy is perhaps the most successful effort I have ever been privileged to be a part of. As I write this in August of 2009, 464 students are registered for the 2009-10 school year in grades k-8. It is the source of continuing satisfaction and pride.

Reading to students at the New Spirit School

At Grand Opening of the Seven Hills Classical Academy

CHAPTER XII

TRAVELS

Much have I travel'd in the realms of gold,
And many goodly states and kingdoms seen;
Round many western islands have I been
Which bards in fealty to Apolo hold.

                                          John Keats

In the summer of 1990 J.S. was twenty-two and was working full time at the country club as a caddie master, and Shannon went to Jamestown to visit her grandparents and cousins. The idea of staying at home by myself and watching TV was not a pleasant one. Hence I decided to go to Greece. A colleague from St. Catherine's had put me in touch with a tour company that was giving classics professors a discount on cruises in the Aegean in the hopes that they would bring groups of students on future cruises. Everything worked out fine, and I flew off to Athens.

Much to my chagrin, when I contacted the officials at the travel agency in Athens, I was told that the cruise had been canceled because the sea was too rough. Thus I had a week or two in Athens by myself with little to do but go sightseeing. Of course, for the classicist there is no more exciting place in the world than Athens, and I had only been there once before in 1967. Still Athens is very hot in August, and the air quality can be bad if there isn't a breeze from the sea. I was staying at the American School of Classical Studies, and fortunately I had noticed a poster in the lobby announcing a conference on the philosophy of Socrates on the island of Samos. I decided to go. It was one of the best things I ever did, and it changed my life and especially my career. At the first session I saw immediately that this was the type of conference at which I could give a paper. Greece has something we don't have in the United States—there are people whose hobby is philosophy. It is not unusual in Greece to have a retired architect or pharmacist or a chemical engineer or even the mayor of the local town or the governor of the island give a paper at a philosophical conference. There are also people trained in philosophy who are philosophers or at least devotees of philosophy who do not have academic positions but support themselves with grants, living most likely very simply which, of course, is entirely appropriate for a "lover of wisdom." In the U.S., on the other hand, almost all philosophers are professors of philosophy, and papers which are delivered at conferences tend to be highly technical especially since philosophy in the U.S. is dominated by champions of analytic philosophy. An amateur of philosophy would never get on the program of a philosophical meeting in the United States or England for that matter.

I am a professional philologist and only an amateur philosopher even though I've devoted most of my time and energy to Greek philosophy for the past twenty to twenty-five years. After observing the kind of papers that were given in Greece, I submitted an abstract for the following summer's conference, and I've given a paper in Greece every summer since and sometimes, in fact, two papers. These summer conferences changed my life and my career for many reasons; for example, they gave me deadlines that I had to meet. At the end of each meeting the honorary presidents meet with Professor Boudouris, the founder and organizer of the International Association for Greek Philosophy (IAGP hereafter), to decide the topic for the following year. Abstracts of proposed papers are due February 1. I usually spend the month of January doing reading and research for the abstract and for my paper. Papers are published in the proceedings of each conference which are for sale at the following year's conference. This schedule meshed perfectly with my teaching duties at Macalester which, by the way, has a special fund for faculty members who are giving papers at international conferences. At the time I retired I held the record for the number of grants received although someone else received more money *in toto* than I did.

Thanks to these conferences I have approximately thirty scholarly publications each of which also resulted in a salary increase. In the year 2002 I was made an honorary president of the IAGP and hence play a role in evaluating conferences and planning future ones. I also receive part of my expenses if the organizer has been successful in raising enough funds. I shudder to think where my career would have gone without these summer gatherings in Greece. As will be seen by the readers who persevere, about one half of our conferences have been held on the island of Samos and the other one half have been on other islands such as Rhodes, Cos, Lesbos,

Spetsis, Crete, etc., and we met twice in Macedonia. When possible the site of the conference has something to do with the theme, e.g., when we met on Cos, a center for the Hippocratic School of Medicine in antiquity, the topic was "Philosophy and Medicine," and when we met on Lesbos, the topic was "Philosophy and Art." The two times we met in Macedonia we were near Stagira, the birthplace of Aristotle.

Something happened at the second conference in 1991 which gives me great pleasure to recall. I met a very special person, a beautiful young Greek girl who against all odds became a wonderful friend of mine, Assimina Strongili ("Meni" to her friends). Meni was a student in philosophy at the University of Athens, and she was working at the registration desk at the 1991 conference. Minutes before the banquet on the opening night I went to the desk and asked her if she was working there, and she said. "Ya." I then asked if there was going to be a banquet, and she answered, "Ya." I asked if it was starting soon, and she answered, "Ya." I then asked her if she spoke English and she said, "Ya." I asked her if she knew any English words besides "Ya," and she said, "Ya." By this time we were sharing a good laugh. Finally I asked her if she knew where the banquet was to be held, and she replied that, in fact, nobody knew. (This is not as unusual as it might sound at a meeting in Greece.) So the two of us set out to find the banquet hall. We sat together at the dinner, and strange as it may seem, we were inseparable for the rest of the five-day conference. Returning from an excursion on Patmos by hydrofoil, she fell asleep with her head on my shoulder. I am her father's age, but in spite of the generation gap "we hit it off." Many young people in Greece are fascinated by Americans and by America, but it wasn't that Meni wanted to come to the U.S. After the conference we became "pen pals," and we've met every summer since 1991 with the sole exception of 2008 when a strike by workers at Olympic Airways forced Mary Ann and me to change our schedule and miss our meeting with Meni.

One summer when she didn't have a job, she showed me around Athens, and another summer I met her on Santorini where she was visiting friends. I rented a jeep, and she gave me a guided tour of that beautiful island for three days. Santorini is crescent shaped being part of the rim of a volcano. In antiquity it was known as Thera, and its eruption may have caused the downfall of the Minoan civilization on Crete. It's a very beautiful and interesting island. After Mary Ann and I got married, we continued to visit Meni each summer, and we have followed her career as she married her husband, Apostoli, gave birth to a son (Ilias), and has flourished in her job with a Greek foundation that promotes Greek art and culture. Meni, who sees life as a miracle and a gift, has brought much happiness, joy and love to our lives.

At the risk of boring readers the rest of this long chapter describes briefly the conferences we've attended in Greece and some of the papers I've given. After Mary Ann and I were married in 1994 we combined trips to Greece with two-week vacation trips to other places. Mary Ann, meanwhile, also has become an insider at these conferences being a very close friend of the organizer's wife and many of the regulars and their wives which, of course, has enhanced my standing in the organization.

During the summer of 1991 I also spent some days on Crete visiting a friend from the University of Minnesota, an archaeologist who was supervising a mountaintop dig at a place called Kavousi. Checking some records I found that that summer I paid the $15 per night for my room at the American School. I paid $9.00 per night at a pension on Crete; a big meal in 1991 with wine cost $7.00; a long taxi cab ride $2.50. Today (2009) one would have to multiply those figures by ten except perhaps the cost of the meal.

In the early 1990s I also attended some conferences organized by Professor Bargeliotis of the University of Athens. His conferences were held at ancient Olympia, and in 1991 the topic was "The Role of Philosophy in the Unification of Europe." I don't recall any of the papers, but I doubt that philosophy played much of a role in the creation of the European Union.

In 1992 I gave my first paper at the IAGP conference on Rhodes. The title was "Stoic Attitudes towards the Contemplative Life," a topic that attracted me because I knew that in the Middle Ages the various religious orders had disputes about whether the *vita contemplativa* was superior to the *vita activa* or vice versa. I was also curious to see what ancient Greek philosophers had said about contemplation and meditation since these are usually associated with Oriental religions and philosophies. I might add here that I have often given papers on subjects I knew little about but wanted to explore. This practice called for months of research and resulted in papers with many footnotes, something about which editors have occasionally chided me.

In 1993 I proposed a paper on "Orthodoxy, Hellenization, and Dehellenization," and much to my surprise I was chosen to deliver it as the first paper at the opening session. Professor Boudouris even translated my paper into modern Greek and read it to a group of monks during an excursion to the island of Patmos. This meeting took place on Samos and was especially enjoyable and memorable because our friends the Sullivans also attended.

To digress for a moment I should point out that in Europe the Greeks are famous for their hospitality and that the conferences we attend usually last a week and involve a good deal of dancing, drinking, singing, and feasting. It is usual for the local mayor or governor of the island (and once even the bishop) and always Professor Boudouris to host a banquet complete with huge amounts of *hors d'oeuvres*, main dishes, desserts, and so forth. There is normally a beach party, and an excursion to another island or a tour of the hosting island. All of this together with the chance to exchange ideas, argue (rationally of course), meet old friends, and make new ones have made these conferences high points in our lives.

To return to my paper on "Hellenization and Dehellenization," my interest in the topic grew out of discussions in a course called "Athens and Jerusalem" I taught for thirteen years with a colleague from the Religion Department. The issue was whether the hellenization of Christianity, that is, the expression of Christian beliefs in Greek philosophical terms had distorted Christianity or if, on the contrary, Greek thinkers such as Plato and Aristotle had discovered truths of perennial value, and hellenization only made explicit some truths that were implicit in the Bible. The Greeks were pleased to hear me defend the latter position. In the course of my research I learned also that the Orthodox call themselves Orthodox because they think that the rest of us Christians are unorthodox!

Before the 1993 conference Mary Ann, Shannon and I went to the Holy Land. Prior to leaving we had lunch with Rabbi Raskas who taught at Macalester and had an apartment in Jerusalem where he went each summer. He recommended an inn run by Notre Dame nuns where there were also Spanish pilgrims, French pilgrims, German pilgrims, and others who were singing hymns daily which added greatly to the religious experience of visiting the various holy sites. Highlights outside of Jerusalem included swimming in the Dead Sea and visiting Masada where Jews committed suicide *en masse* in 73 A.D. rather than surrender to the Romans. The visit to the Holy Land affected the three of us profoundly although none of us suffered or succumbed to the "Jerusalem syndrome," which has been observed since the Middle Ages. Some pilgrims, overwhelmed by the religious experience, become almost psychotic. Fortunately these spells are normally of short duration.

Istanbul, 1994

The sixth IAGP conference was held in Ierissos in August of 1994. The theme was "Aristotelian Political Thought" and my paper was entitled "Aristotle, Education, and the Multicultural Society." Ierissos was chosen because of its proximity to Stagira, the birthplace of Aristotle, which we visited. After the conference Mary Ann and I decided to take the train to Xanthi, a city in Thrace which was on the route to Istanbul, our ultimate goal. We stopped there for a couple of days to visit a friend, George Pavlos whom I had met at previous conferences. Unfortunately George had been called to Salonica to appear on television so his poor wife was obliged to entertain us. Since she spoke no English, and we didn't speak modern Greek, there were some amusing moments, but she gave us a walking tour of the city, entertained us in her home, and introduced us to some of their friends. She had three young sons who were running around the house. Whenever one of them passed by close enough, she'd give him a whack even if he wasn't misbehaving. I assumed it was something like "preventive maintenance."

From Xanthi we went by train to Istanbul. At the station in Xanthi there were people who could speak English, and as usual they were eager to talk to Americans. They could not believe that Americans were taking the train to Istanbul. When we got to our compartment, we understood why they were surprised. It appeared that the train hadn't been cleaned for years. The curtains were too grimy to touch. We didn't want to lean our heads on the back of the seats. Finally we put plastic bags over our heads so we could lean back. It was an all-night train ride (we were younger then). Part of the time I slept with my head on Mary Ann's lap, and then we switched around. The ride was uneventful except for a couple of incidents. At one point a man entered our compartment and asked if we had change for a $20 bill. I said, "No," and I'm glad I did since he might have been checking to see where I kept my money.

In the middle of the night we were joined by three Muslim women and girl. We knew they were talking about us, and finally the young girl who spoke some English asked if we were Bulgarians! (We were near the Bulgarian border.) When we replied that we were Americans, they were obviously amazed and delighted.

Istanbul was full of surprises. First of all, our hotel was French, and everything was in French including prices in the souvenir shop and on the menu. Over the years I had studied a good deal of French, and it came in handy especially since we didn't know a word of Turkish except perhaps "shish kebab."

Before the trip when we had told friends in Greece and that we were going to Turkey, they had urged us not to go. We were told that there was a cholera epidemic in Istanbul which the authorities were keeping quiet lest tourists be frightened away. We were also told that not even bottled water was safe to drink in Turkey because the Turks didn't wash the bottles properly. Finally a friend told us that a young woman had flown from Istanbul to Greece and had dropped dead at the Athens airport from something she had caught in Istanbul. (Anyone familiar with modern Greek history knows that there has been no love between Greeks and the Turks for at least 400 years.) Hence we were very pleasantly surprised to find that Istanbul is a wonderful city, one of the greatest cities in the world, full of museums and art galleries, churches and mosques, monuments and all the sorts of things that we like to see and visit. Moreover we found the Turks with whom we dealt friendly, kind, honest, charming, and amusing. The food too is excellent, and since the dollar was strong in those days, everything was a bargain. Consequently we ate in some of the best restaurants in Istanbul. There was, however, one untoward incident. My billfold was stolen from my back pocket. We were walking in a crowded street after supper one evening when a man ahead of us suddenly began slapping a boy and pushing him against me. While I was fending them all off, an accomplice behind us took my billfold from my pocket. Actually all of my money and my credit cards were in a pouch which I carried around my neck, and the billfold was a decoy stuffed with pieces of newspaper. It was a practice I had started in Italy, and it worked a couple of other times too.

I'll say nothing about the specific sites in Istanbul, but a couple of events come to mind. One was a late night, very romantic dinner Mary Ann and I had on the roof of the hotel from which we watched the lights of ships sailing through the Dardanelles. There was a piano player who sang some songs in English, but one had the feeling he didn't know what the words meant. Nevertheless it was a delightful and memorable evening. The other very pleasant experience was spending a day with my colleague from Macalester, Michael Schneider, who had been teaching computer science in Istanbul for some months and knew the city well. He took us through the Grand Bazaar, an unforgettable experience, and then down through the Dardanelles by public boat to visit a crusader castle and the site of the Battle of Gallipoli (World War I, 1915), a tragedy which was powerfully portrayed by the 1981 Australian movie of the same title. We loved Istanbul and resolved to return which we did as readers who persevere will see.

Turkey, 1995

Since we enjoyed our visit to Turkey so much in 1994, we decided to spend more time there in 1995. Samos is only a short ferry ride from Turkey and Ephesus, and many people from the IAGP conference have been known to skip out one day, cross over to Ephesus and spend the day sightseeing, then return in the evening for dinner. Ephesus reminded me of Pompeii except that Pompeii is dry, dusty, and crumbling whereas everything at Ephesus, since it was made of marble (even the streets), is clean and bright. We spent most of the day there going from temple to temple and from the library to the amphitheater, to private dwellings and so forth.

From Ephesus we went to Izmir. Our hotel was across the street from the Hilton, and everywhere there were signs saying "house running." At first we thought it was a typo for "horse running" but then we saw people actually doing it at the Hilton. For a modest fee a person could go up to the roof, run down the front of the hotel to the sidewalk attached to a rope coming over a pulley on the roof. It was "all the rage" in Izmir, but we chose not to try it. We signed up for a tour which took us to Priene, Pergamum, and Miletus, the birthplace of Thales and of philosophy. Much to our surprise we were the only two on the tour and our guide was Jewish although Turkey is 99% Muslim. He was a tall, handsome young man who told us a moving story. When the Jews were expelled from Spain in 1492, Turkey was the only country that would take them. That is how our guide's ancestors got to Turkey where his family has lived for over 500 years. The Jews in Turkey speak a language called Ladino which is a mixture of old Spanish, Hebrew and to a lesser extent Turkish and Greek. He also told us that his family has keys to the houses their ancestors occupied in Spain; they have passed them down from generation to generation since 1942. He had relatives in the United States including a brother whom he wanted to visit. Unfortunately the Turkish officials would not allow him to leave the country for fear he might not return. The Turks were fighting the Kurds in eastern Turkey, and he thought, because he was tall and husky, the government wanted to draft him and send him to the front lines.

From there we made our way to Canakkale, a modern city near what is thought to be the site of Troy. Since I had discussed *The Iliad, The Odyssey,* and the story of the Trojan war for over twenty-five years in various classes, and since I had a special interest in Heinrich Schliemann, the man given credit for locating and excavating Troy, it was a thrill to spend most of a day studying the ruins. Mary Ann took a nice picture of me in the Trojan horse which the Turks have built for the tourists.

From Troy we went by bus to Istanbul, and it was an unforgettable experience. It was a double-decker bus similar to the ones found in London, and it had a stewardess. A couple of times during the day-long journey she came around with a plastic spray bottle full of perfumed water. The first time I shook my head and indicated with my hands that I didn't want perfumed water sprayed on them, but she insisted. It was apparently required. Once everyone's hands had been properly cleaned, she came around with cookies. There was no bathroom on board, and the bus only stopped every two hours so it's just as well we weren't served anything to drink. We were sitting near the back of the bus, and I noticed that the whole backseat was empty—it was wide enough for five people. Hence I decided to take a nap. I moved back and stretched out. No sooner had I gotten comfortable, than a gentleman in uniform, whom I assumed worked for the bus company, arrived and signaled for me to move back to my seat which I promptly did. He then stretched out and took a nap himself.

Early in the afternoon the bus suddenly stopped at a gas station literally "in the middle of nowhere," and everyone got off, the driver removed everyone's luggage from under the bus, set it on the ground, and drove off. We were totally mystified and not a little upset. There seem to be no one around who spoke English. Finally we found a Danish couple whose English was excellent. They assured us that another bus would come fairly soon and take us the rest of the way which is exactly what happened. The couple were on their fourth trip to Turkey. They explained why they liked the country: the people are kind and honest, there is a lot to see, and everything is a bargain. That was our experience too.

When we got near Istanbul, we discovered that the bus didn't actually go into town; it stopped at what might be called a "busport." From there one had to take a taxi or tram into the city. While we were figuring out what to do, a man came up with a two-wheeled cart and offered to take us to a taxi. The car he took us to was yellow, and it resembles a taxi, but it didn't have a taxi sign on the roof. We probably should not have taken it, but the two young men in the front seat looked honest. Once on the way, the guy who was sitting in the front beside the driver turned around, showed us a brochure, and said, "Come to our hotel," which was about the extent of his English. I said "No" and tried to explain that we had a reservation at a hotel whose address was on the card I had given the driver. But he insisted that we go to their hotel. I decided I would try to "butter them up" a bit. I told him we loved Turkey so much that we had returned a second time, and that we loved the Turkish people too. Our friend turned around and said simply, "We are Kurds." As indicated earlier the Turks and the Kurds were fighting a war in eastern Turkey. So much for "buttering them up."

As we got into town, it became obvious that they didn't know their way around. They only knew the route from the busport to their hotel. Finally I saw Santa Sophia and knew that our hotel was nearby. I told the driver to stop which he did, and I got out and demanded our suitcases. The driver said, "One million lire!" By this time another driver who could speak English had come over. I asked him if there were tourist police in Istanbul. Our driver apparently heard the word "police" since he said immediately, "One half million lire" which was a reasonable price so I paid him, and they departed, thanks be to God. We figured they were young Kurds who had come to Istanbul, perhaps illegally, found a job with a hotel picking up passengers from buses and were still learning their way around town. Through it all we never felt we were in danger.

Our new driver turned out to be a colorful character. He claimed to be the world's most famous taxi driver. Before putting the car into gear, he showed us his scrapbook which was full of pictures of him with celebrities. He wanted us to hire him by the day so he could show us the town. We just wanted to get to our hotel. When we finally arrived there, we got red carpet treatment since the bell boys were surprised and amazed that we remember them and their names from our previous visit. The rest of the visit was uneventful and was spent as usual—visiting museums, art galleries, monuments, etc. with some shopping, eating out, and relaxing for variety.

Italy, 1996

In 1996 following the eighth IAGP conference Mary Ann and I spent a couple of weeks in Italy. From my standpoint it was the most difficult of all our trips since we were constantly packing and unpacking, catching taxis to train stations, trying to find the right train, etc. On that trip we, or at least I, realized that such a tour is fine for college kids, but it's better for senior citizens to go to one place, settle down in a hotel for a week or so, and make excursions from there.

We took the train from Athens to Patras which was uneventful and pleasant, but the adventures begin once we were on the pier from which the ferry left for Brindisi in Italy. The ferry was scheduled to leave at 6:00 PM and arrive the next morning. We were dropped off about half a mile from the ship and told that a pickup would come to fetch us and our luggage. As 6:00 PM approached, we began to get more nervous; in fact, I have never seen Mary Ann so nervous. Finally the pickup arrived, but the driver seemed to be in no hurry. When we finally got to the ferry, we discovered that everyone else knew something we didn't know—it was not going to leave on time. In fact, it didn't leave until 9:00 PM. (It's called "Greek time.")

When we were finally allowed to go on board, we had to carry our own luggage up a narrow winding staircase. Then we discovered that the dining room, the lounges, and the bar were not yet open because the computers were down. I finally got permission to leave the ship to buy some soft drinks and sandwiches from a kiosk on the pier. As we ate our sandwiches and drank our pop in the bar that was still not open for business, other starving passengers stared at us enviously. Once we got into our cabin we slept well being exhausted from the long train ride and the longer wait.

In Brindisi we had an even more interesting adventure. We were left on the pier, and every one else quickly disappeared. We needed to get to the train station and get tickets for the trip to Rome. Finally I spotted a travel agency with a sign over the entrance saying "*Biglietti—Roma.*" Once inside I noticed that only one window was staffed and there was a long line at it. There were other windows, but no agents were at them. I went to one of the empty windows, nevertheless, hoping that someone might come from the backroom and sell us our tickets. Instead the man who was working at the window with a long line left them and came over to wait on me. "He had seen us coming," as the saying goes. I asked how much two one-way tickets to Rome would cost, and he gave the price in dollars, $50.00 even, which I thought a bit odd. I asked if he would take a traveler's check, and he said that actually they preferred travelers checks. I asked if I should fill in the payee line, and he said they had a rubber stamp for that. So we were given our tickets, and I gave him the $50.00 travelers check. I then asked where we could catch a taxi, and much to my surprise, he said that he would take us to the train station. (Meanwhile someone else had come from the backroom to wait on those in line.) When I expressed surprise that he had offered to drive us to the train station, he explained that he had several children and whenever he could make a little extra money by driving tourists around he did. We were told to take our suitcases out to the curb and wait for him to pick us up there. He also urged us to hurry since the train would be leaving soon.

Once at the *stazione* I paid the fare and, according to Mary Ann, even gave him a tip. Inside we discovered that the train wasn't scheduled to leave for several hours. Later when we were on our way, I was reading our receipt, and I realized what our friend, the driver, had done. At the bottom of the receipt he had written in Italian "Paid in cash X number of lire. I don't remember the exact amount, but it was considerably less than $50. Apparently after dropping us off, he'd gone to the bank, put his own name on the payee line of the travelers check, cashed it, returned to the travel agency where he put the correct amount in the cash register and pocketed the difference. I would have been angry, but it hadn't been a large amount, and furthermore I had to admire his ingenuity.

In Rome we stayed in a pension a run by nuns from Lebanon and visited the usual sites: St. Peter's, the Vatican Museum, the Roman Forum, the Coliseum, Circus Maximus, etc. A special treat was running into Father Foster who made a big fuss over us and invited us to visit his class that afternoon where he introduced me as the founder of his summer program. While in Italy I kept telling Mary Ann I hoped we would see a good argument between at least two Italians; it can be quite a sight. Fortunately it happened on a bus when one man accused another of pushing his wife.

Taking the train to Florence, we checked into another pension run by nuns and visited the most important museums, churches, art galleries, etc. of that most charming of cities. Also in Italy and elsewhere we allotted a good deal of time to just sitting at sidewalk cafes, "people watching," reading, and relaxing. For our visit to Venice we stayed in a small town nearby and took the tram into Venice each day. Everything about Venice is charming, and our visit was one long aesthetic experience which had been true of Florence too.

In Turin we visited our old and dear friends Aldo and Laura and their son, Ludovico, who at the time was only three or four. Laura fixed some memorable meals for us. One evening they took us out to dinner at their favorite restaurant for the *specialita della casa* which was steak tartar, that is raw hamburger! I wasn't going to even taste it, but I did after I saw them giving it to Ludovico who ate it eagerly. We flew home from the Milan exhausted but happy. I, however, resolved never to try to cover so many cities and do so much sightseeing in a two-week period.

Rhodes and Turkey, 1997

Following the conference on Cos in 1997, Mary Ann and I spent a restful week on Rhodes with several day trips to Turkey to visit such sites as Halicarnassis (modern Bodrum), hometown of the Greek historian Herodotus and site of King Mausoleus' tomb, one of the seven wonders of the ancient world.

Greece and Turkey, 1998

August 1998 was one of the busiest months of our life. I'm not quite sure how we did it. From August 2 to 5 we attended a conference at ancient Olympia. On August 6 we went to Athens, and the next day we picked up a rental car and spent five days driving around northern Greece (Volos, Kalambaka, Meteora, Pelio). On the 12th we flew from Athens to the island of Samos where we stayed in the Doyssa Bay Hotel, site of many IAGP conferences, whence the next day we went to Kusadasi, Turkey and then to Izmir where we met our driver who drove us around western Turkey for a week (details below). On the 23rd it was back to Samos for the 10th annual IAGP conference which lasted until the 28th.

I should explain first that besides the IAGP conferences organized by Professor Boudouris there were other conferences on Greek philosophy arranged by another faculty member from the University of Athens whom I will call Professor X. Professor X's conferences were notoriously disorganized, and the 1998 meeting set a new record for chaos. The first time the conference was announced, the registration fee was given as $500 which was twice what it had been the previous year. I sent him an e-mail message complaining. He replied, "Don't worry. Just come and we'll negotiate something." Some weeks later I sent another message asking how much it would cost for Mary Ann as an accompanying person. He replied, "Don't worry; it's negotiable just come and we'll negotiate something." As I was writing my paper, I began to wonder how long I would have to present it—fifteen minutes, twenty minutes, a half hour, or what. In reply to my message regarding the amount of time I would have, he wrote, "It's flexible and it depends upon the person who is chairing the session." When I asked who that would be, he replied, "You can't find out until you arrive."

The first two days of the conference went reasonably well, but on the morning of the third day there was an announcement on the P.A. system telling us to pack up and put our luggage on the bus; we were going on an excursion. In itself this was not unusual since, as I may have mentioned before, conferences in Greece usually include a one-day excursion to a historical site or another island. The bus took us to a village called Lechina on the route to Athens where we had a session in a room over a bank. The room was small and crowded and lacked air conditioning on a day that was very hot. What was most memorable, however, was that the white plastic chairs we were sitting on kept breaking. Every so often there would be a crash, and another philosopher would hit the floor.

After lunch it was announced that nothing was scheduled until 8:00 PM that evening when there would be readings from various Greek tragedies in the ruins of a local theater. The afternoon was free, and there were three things we could do: go swimming, take a tour of the city (which would have taken about a half-hour), or take a nap in the home of a local resident. I favored the latter, but no arrangements had been made, and we didn't want to go from house to house asking if they had a bed or sofa where we were we could take a nap. That left swimming, but the bus driver would not let people take their luggage out to get their swimming suits. Hence we walked to the beach where some went swimming in their underwear, and others took naps on the beach. After the performance at the theater that evening which most found very boring, we went to an upscale restaurant where we did have a wonderful dinner at about 11 o'clock at night. As elegant as the restaurant was and as excellent as the food was, it wasn't enough to assuage the anger of many, especially those attending a conference in Greece for the first time. After the dinner the bus returned us to a hotel in Olympia; it was nearly 4:00 A.M. when we got to bed. Apparently Professor X had failed to negotiate enough money from the participants, and the whole conference had been kicked out of the Olympic Village! We were told to be by the curb at 8:00 AM for the bus ride to Athens. Mary Ann and I were there promptly at the appointed time, but no one else was, not even the bus driver. He finally arrived about a half hour late—more "Greek time." It was without a doubt the world's most disorganized conference.

On the 7th we picked up a rental car in Athens and drove to Volos, the ancient city from which Jason sailed with the Argonauts to fetch the golden fleece. After visiting the local sites, we drove next day to Kalambaka where we visited Meteora where there are column-like mountains on the top of which there are monasteries and in one case a convent. These are clearly places for people who want to get away from earth and be as close to heaven as possible. Among the other famous sites that we visited in the area was Mount Pelion where Chiron, the learned centaur had tutored Achilles according to Greek mythology. On the 11th we return to Athens and flew to Samos. The next day we took the ferry to Kusadasi, Turkey whence we made our way by bus to Izmir.

Many colleges in the United States organize tours for their alumni. During our previous visits to Turkey, I had been struck by the amount of Greek history and Greek mythology that took place, not in Greece proper, but in what is today western Turkey. In antiquity this was known as Ionia and included many great Greek cities such as Miletus, Ephesus, and Halicarnassus. Troy too was located in the northwest corner of Ionia. Since I had been teaching classical mythology for many years, it occurred to me that I could lead a very good classical tour to Turkey for our alumni. The Alumni Office agreed, and I was lucky enough to find a Turkish travel agency that was interested in making the arrangements. They provided us with a car and driver for a week to visit sites and work out an itinerary. Our only expense would be a tip for the driver. He turned out to be a very charming young man named Baha whose English was good and who was passionately interested in mythology. Hence I entertained him as we drove from site to site with stories about Greek gods and heroes. We visited such ancient cities as Nyssa, Aphrodisias, Hieropolis, Myra, Perge and Antalya.

One day for lunch Baha took us on a hike up a mountain to a site known as "Chimera" where fire comes up from cracks in the earth. (It's natural gas that has been burning for many years.) He had brought some sausages, and we roasted them on the fire and had a very nice picnic. The last few days went by rather quickly since on August 20 President Clinton sent bombers to bomb what turned out to be a pharmaceutical factory in Khartoum, Sudan in retaliation for attacks on U.S. embassies in Africa and also, as we learned later, in an attempt to kill Osama bin Laden. Baha thought that Americans might not be safe in certain Muslim cities in that part of Turkey so we returned quickly to Izmir. From there we went back to Samos for the IAGP conference on "Philosophy and Ecology." That conference lasted from August 23 to the 28th, and then we flew home. Back at Macalester I learned that the Alumni Office had dropped plans for a mythological tour of Turkey deeming it to risky for Americans at that time.

Egypt, 1999

Almost everyone dreams about visiting Egypt. At least I had for many years. In 1999 Mary Ann and I decided to do it. A year or so earlier I had met a Macalester alumnus named Craig Olson at an annual alumni reunion. He was working in Cairo on a project designed to improve the quality of the city's drinking water. He had offered to help us plan at tour of Egypt if we ever came there. Naturally I contacted him during the winter of 1999. His advice was to get plane tickets to and from Cairo, reserve a hotel room there, and after our arrival he would help us with the rest of the visit. I had discovered that the Marriott Hotel in Cairo had a special for senior citizens; I think the rate was an incredible $67 per night. Hence I made a reservation.

When we arrived at the Cairo airport, it was about two o'clock in the morning. We had to fight our way through a throng of taxicab drivers all of whom wanted to deliver us to the Marriott. We finally chose the one who was shouting out the lowest fare. Once at the desk of the hotel around three o'clock in the morning, the clerk informed us that there were no rooms left. As my heart was sinking, he added, "And so we're going to have to give you a suite for the price of a room." Our suite consisted of a large foyer, a living room with two sofas, two balconies overlooking the Nile, two TV sets, a dining room, and a separate bedroom shut off by French doors. The bathroom was huge with a marble floor and marble walls. The sign on the door said "$400 per night," and on one of the TV sets there was a card that said "Have a whole lamb roasted in your room for $300."

We expected to be moved to a typical room the next day; instead they let us stay there for four nights! Each day the maid brought us a bowl of fruit, and each evening she came in to turn the covers down for us. We later learned that every floor had one such suite and that Hillary Clinton and her daughter had stayed in one of them a week or so before our arrival. (I should mention that the Cairo Marriott consists of a former royal palace with two towers added by the Marriott people to make it a five star hotel. In addition there were six acres of gardens, a swimming pool, casino and all the other amenities one could desire including five or six restaurants.)

Being an early riser, I went down for breakfast around 7:00 AM and discovered that there were very few Westerners staying in the hotel. As I told Mary Ann after breakfast, it looked like a convention of OPEC ministers. Craig told us later that the Saudis came to Cairo in August because it's cooler there -110° instead of 120°. Needless to say we were tempted to simply stay in our beautiful suite and look out the window at the Nile and other sites that were nearby, but we met with Craig who made a list of museums, mosques, pyramids, etc. for us to see before taking our cruise on the Nile. He also made arrangements with a taxicab driver he knew to drive us around town the first day (for a very reasonable price) while we were getting our bearings. Before leaving home I had asked a student we had from Egypt about public transportation in Cairo. She said simply, "Take taxis." I soon discovered why she was so curt. Public transportation in Cairo that I saw consisted of Toyota pickups equipped with bars for passengers to hold on as they stood in the back. Some passengers even stood on the rear bumper. There were two types of taxis in Cairo, "street taxis" and "hotel taxis" the latter of which are called limousines. They are all Toyotas and are all the same size; hotel taxis are just newer and cleaner and are parked near hotels

One day we visited the great pyramid of Cheops, one of three pyramids near Cairo in what is called the "Giza Necropolis." It had recently been opened to the public. Being a gentleman, I let Mary Ann enter first and I followed. As the passage way became narrower and lower so that one had to duck down, I had the worst attack of claustrophobia of my life. I had visions of an earthquake occurring, causing rocks to slide so that we were trapped inside. Never have I made such a speedy exit from anything in my life. Mary Ann persevered and visited the innermost chambers. I will not describe the experience further for fear of a panic attack. In the evening we watched the sound and light show at the pyramids which is spectacular and very well worth seeing. One thing, however, was a bit incongruous. Behind us across the street from the pyramids was a Pizza Hut.

One can rent a car in Cairo; Hertz, Avis, etc. all have offices there, but Americans are advised to hire a driver also. The traffic in Cairo is even more chaotic than in Rome and Athens. There were police at many intersections, but drivers ignored them, made fun of them, and tried to slip by behind them. Also Egypt is the only country I've been in where the official government tourist bureau advises tourists not to eat in local restaurants. Fortunately at the Marriott there were several good restaurants. Our favorite was an English pub where the food was excellent and beer never tasted better.

Most people who visit Egypt take a cruise on the Nile which is what we did. There are two ways to do it. One can start in Cairo sail up the Nile to Luxor and then fly back to Cairo, or one can fly to Luxor and then sail down the Nile to Cairo. (The Nile flows northward.) We chose the first option. I think we were the only Americans on the ship, and we were given the best cabinet on the boat—right in the bow. Most likely the crew thought we would tip the most. (I'm sure they were disappointed.) We spent most of the time with a couple from India, three Filipino girls, and a young Englishman who was taking his son on a holiday. Most of the other passengers were Italians and Spaniards.

In addition to visiting sites along the way, there was entertainment in the evenings—belly dancers, whirling dervishes, and one night a masquerade ball. The latter was a money-making scheme for the tour company since they conveniently opened a shop the day before the ball and rented costumes. We managed, however, to outfox them. I went ashore and got a branch from a bush to wear around my head as a wreath and took a sheet from our bed and made a toga out of it. I went to the ball as Julius Caesar, and Mary Ann used a headscarf as a veil and was Cleopatra. On the last day of the cruise we spent the afternoon touring the Valley of the Queens where the temperature was well above 100. That night was the masquerade ball which lasted until the wee hours of the morning. I recall telling Mary Ann I was surprised that we, or at least I, wasn't exhausted at all. I felt great. When we got to our air-conditioned hotel the next morning at Luxor, however, we collapsed on the bed and didn't get up for nearly twelve hours. After flying back to Cairo we spent a few more days at the Marriott in a more modest room and spent one day in Alexandria before heading home.

Egypt is of special interest to classicists for many reasons. First of all ancient Egyptian history, art, architecture, religion, and culture in general with its Old Kingdom, New Kingdom, and Late Kingdom are supremely fascinating. Then the Greeks ruled Egypt from Alexander the Great's conquest of it in 320 B.C. until Cleopatra's death in 30 B.C. when the Romans took over. It was fascinating to see in the art, architecture, religion, and mythology the mingling of these three great cultures.

I had not heard of "*baksheesh*" before going to Egypt. One day we decided to visit a famous mosque. First of all it was a surprise me that we had to buy tickets to gain entrance. I gave the man selling tickets the money, and he returned the change, but instead of sliding the tickets out to me, as I expected, he kept sliding them back-and-forth as if he were playing a shell game. I was thoroughly mystified. Finally I realized that he expected a tip, i.e. *baksheesh*. Only after I gave them some coins did he finally give us our tickets. Another day in a Christian museum the guard joined us as we walked around. His English was very limited, but he insisted on giving us a guided tour. His comments were limited to statements such as "That's Jesus" and "Over there is Mary" and so forth. As we were about to leave he began to salute me. I was amazed, and I said to Mary Ann, "Look, he's saluting us." When he realized I didn't get it, he began lowering his arm after each salute and turning his palm up. That I understood.

Our last day in Egypt was spent in Alexandria which was one of the most famous cities in classical antiquity, having been founded in 334 B.C. by Alexander the Great. We visited the site of the famous library (they were just opening a new library there), the site of the lighthouse, one of the seven wonders of the ancient world, the Roman amphitheater, the catacombs, and the palace that was once used by King Farouk. We were blessed to have a wonderful guide who didn't simply lecture at the sites but dramatized each presentation. The next day we flew back to Amsterdam and from there to home, somewhat exhausted but also uplifted and inspired with renewed enthusiasm for study of the ancient world.

South Africa, 2000

At the conferences in Greece we have made many wonderful friends from all over the world, but none were closer or more dear than the Gerickes from South Africa. John is an ordained minister and was a professor of philosophy at Pretoria where his wife, Elizabeth, was a librarian and professor of Library Science. The four of us were inseparable at dinners and parties, and John and I even used to dance together which isn't unusual for men to do in Greece. In the summer of 2000 John and his colleagues organized a conference on Nietzsche in Pretoria, and Mary Ann and I attended.

We stayed in a wonderful old Dutch mansion. Included in the charge for a room was transportation around town in the inn's van since it wasn't safe to walk in many parts of Pretoria even during the day. We did, however, walk around the university campus which seemed perfectly safe. There were many other aspects of life in Pretoria which were new and troubling to us. For instance, if one parked a car downtown to go shopping, it was necessary to pay one of the men who hung out there to guard the car lest it be vandalized. We drove through beautiful suburbs full of lovely homes, but they all had walls around them, and many had razor wire, guard dogs, and signs saying "Armed Response."

After the conference one of Gericke's friends, "Fannie," (short for Stephan), who had lost his job in insurance and had purchased a Volkswagen van and become a tourist guide, drove us around the Kruger National Park, the largest game preserve in South Africa. It was a unique and memorable experience. Each morning Fannie would find out from the park rangers where the elephants and other animals were and then drive us there for a close-up look. There were hippos, rhino, zebras, giraffes, lions, and various other cats, assorted primates (in addition to humans), wildebeests, hyenas, impalas, etc. In the evenings we sat around a bonfire on which Fannie who was a good cook, fixed supper. The only thing we lacked was someone to play a guitar. We slept in round structures that were made of concrete walls up to six feet or so, and then had thatched roofs above that. Early in the morning we could hear the hippos grunting and snorting in a nearby river. After our week in the Kroger the Gerickes returned to their home, and Fannie drove Mary Ann and me to Cape Town where we saw such sites as Table Mountain, watched the whales off Cape Point, visited caves with prehistoric paintings, a famous botanical Garden, and other places of interest to tourists. This was a vacation that had everything: dear friends, beautiful scenery, good food, good wine and beer, unique experiences plus a chance to learn about a wonderful country although one with challenges of daunting complexity.

Cyprus, 2001

In 2001, thanks to an invitation from a former student, we went to Cyprus. We had thought of going to India but feared it might be too hot there in July and August. It could not have been hotter than Cyprus which is by far the hottest place we have ever been—hotter than Egypt and the Holy Land. It's said that Cyprus has nine months of summer and three of spring. In spite of the heat Cyprus is a very beautiful island, as it should be since it is "Aphrodite's Island."

I knew Cyprus as the place where in the 8th century B.C. Greeks had learned to write from Phoenicians by adapting the Semitic alphabet to Greek. The Semitic peoples, according to the usual account, only represented consonants; the reader had to supply the vowels. The Greeks used some Semitic letters they didn't need for consonants to represent vowels, thus producing the first complete alphabet. The Romans borrowed their alphabet from the Greeks, and we use the Roman one.

Cyprus, because of its location (close to Turkey on the north and Syria on the East) became, as a guide book puts it, "the target of a large number of invaders and conquerors including the Assyrians, the Persians, the Ptolemies of Egypt, the Romans, the Byzantines, Richard "the Lion Heart" of England, the Knights Templar, and the Venetians." From 1571 until 1878 Cyprus was a province of Turkey, and in that year Britain took over.

In 1960 Cyprus finally became independent. In 1974, however, Turkey fearing that the 18% of Cypriots who were Turkish would be disadvantaged if Cyprus united with Greece, invaded and occupied the northern 37% of the territory. Cyprus is unfortunately divided to this day.

Tragic as this history is, it makes Cyprus an interesting place to visit if one is interested in history, archeology, and different cultures. I believe that we visited more archeological sites in Cyprus than anywhere else we have visited. Thanks to my former student and her parents, we were driven into cooler places in the mountains where we visited charming villages and enjoyed some wonderful Cypriot meals and dishes. In 2009, as I write this, we are planning another visit to Cyprus, this time as the site of the 21st annual conference of the IAGP. I expect to spend the days in an air-conditioned hotel and only venture out in the evenings.

China, 2002

In 2002 we decided to go to China after the conference in Greece. Oddly enough we could not get good connections from Greece so we returned to Minnesota and flew to Tokyo and from there to Beijing. At the airport in Beijing we were met by a representative from our tour company, and there was a very pleasant surprise for us: there were only four other persons in our group. Hence we had a guide/interpreter, a driver, and a very nice van for the six of us. The others were the Banks family from Philadelphia, mother, father, and their college-aged son and a daughter. They were perfectly compatible, and we had a wonderful time together.

When we arrived at our hotel, there was another very pleasant surprise. The Chinese government was subsidizing our visit as a part of an effort to lure American tourists to China. Thus we were put up in five-star, ultra-luxurious hotels—everything but gold faucets in the bathrooms. The tour involved visiting three important cities with excursions from each one. I will not bore readers with a list of all the sites. Suffice it to say we visited the most important attractions in each city, for example: the Forbidden City, Tiananmen Square, and the Ming tombs in Beijing. We spent one day at the Great Wall, and it was an unforgettable experience. There were many groups of Chinese from all parts of the country, all wearing a green or blue or red T-shirt or whatever the color of their group was. There was a carnival atmosphere, and people were extremely friendly, charming, and amusing. When I travel in warm climes, I wear a broad brim straw hat on orders from my dermatologist. Although it does not resemble a cowboy hat at all, in my opinion, in both Egypt and China I was thought to be a cowboy. A number of people in China asked to have their picture taken with me. At the Great Wall, however, it was Mary Ann with her blonde hair who was the center of attraction. In fact, she provided some unwanted competition for the owner of a Bactrian camel who is charging people to be photographed with his camel.

Back in Beijing we spent a very pleasant morning in a part of town called the "Hutong" where we were driven around in what one might call a rickshaw only it was drawn by a man on a bicycle instead of a runner. There we saw how local citizens lived: children sitting on the curb brushing their teeth, mothers preparing meals on the Chinese equivalent of a hibachi, and so forth. The only problem was air pollution from all the hibachis. I even had to ask our guide to try to find a face mask for me as I was experiencing shortness of breath. Our guide explained that air pollution is simply the price of industrialization and progress.

A couple of happy memories: One day while Mary Ann was shopping, I sat in a Starbucks reading a book. There were two empty chairs at my table. A young lady came over to me and asked something about a chair which I thought she wanted. I said, "Sure, go ahead." Instead of taking the chair she sat down. She explained that she had studied English for ten years, and all her teachers had been Chinese. She had never spoken to a native speaker of English, and she wanted to know if I would talk with her. It was a delightful experience. She was going to London to visit her uncle and perhaps stay there. Did I think she needed more English lessons? We talked for half an hour or perhaps forty-five minutes. Finally I said I had to return to our hotel to meet my wife and others for supper. She asked if she could walk with me to the hotel which she did, so I had a chance to introduce her to Mary Ann and our friends. Before departing she told us her name in Chinese meant "little fish." What did we think her name should be in English? I said "Minnow" but Mr. Banks had a better suggestion: "Wanda."

As I said, we were extremely lucky to be staying in five-star hotels. Our hotel in Beijing had a Pizza Hut as one of its dining rooms. This Pizza Hut, however, was no ordinary one; it had marble floors, a maître d' and served soup as well as pizza.

From Beijing we went to Xi'an, a city that is least 3100 years old and was the eastern end of the Silk Road. Today Xi'an attracts visitors because of the terra cotta army discovered in 1974 by a farmer who was digging a well. It is estimated that there are 8000 soldiers, 130 chariots, and 670 horses, all life-sized. They were buried with the "First Emperor of Qin" who ruled from 221 to 210 B.C. Each statute is different, and they were originally painted. Considered the greatest archaeological discovery of all time, it is an awesome site which alone would make a trip to China worth the time and expense.

The last city we visited in China was Shanghai. We were told that one half of the cranes in the world were in Shanghai, which is no doubt an example of hyperbole, but it is a booming place. Our guide, who said her father was an official in the Communist Party, called the Chinese economic system "market socialism." "Of course," she said, "it's nothing but capitalism," and I'm sure she approved of it. From our hotel, the most luxurious of all the hotels we stayed in, we could see skyscrapers rising on all sides, and all the major U.S. and international companies were represented. Near our hotel there was an IKEA, and while we were there a Wal-Mart had its grand opening. As Michael Novak has written, God is first and foremost a Creator. Humans are created in the image and likeness of God and are, therefore, called to be creators too. Capitalism is good because it stimulates creativity and a host of other virtues such as ingenuity, prudence, diligence, and cooperation. Communism, on the other hand, as Gorbachev said in Minneapolis, was "an absolute, total, and utter failure. It never worked and never will work." (I've been looking for a chance to plug capitalism. Anyone interested in reading about this subject should get Novak's *The Spirit of Democratic Capitalism* and/or John Paul II's encyclical letter "The Hundredth Year.")

In Shanghai we visited all the principal tourist attractions, including the Shanghai Museum and the Jade Buddha Temple. We were also treated to a performance of the Chinese circus (much like Cirque du Soleil). Most of one day was taken up with an excursion to Suzhou where we visited the "Embroidering Research Institute." Women were working on silk garments, pillows, etc. Each hour they were given a few minutes off to go outside where we observed them doing "eye exercises." I who don't like to shop could not resist the temptation to purchase two silk neckties for $10 each.

I haven't said much about food in Chinese. In Beijing we did have Peking duck. Each serving consists of one half a duck, and it appeared that they had used a band saw to cut from the tip of the beak to the tip of the tail of each duck. We also ate in a restaurant that served forty (or was it eighty?) kinds of dumplings. I liked the government-owned restaurants since the waiters and waitresses refused to accept tips. Capitalism hasn't spread everywhere yet.

From Shanghai we flew to Tokyo where we spent a few hours in the airport. The flight home stands out in my memory because we were bumped up to first class. The trip to South Africa and the trip to China had given us lots of "frequent flyer miles." First class on an international flight means separate reclining chairs, an island loaded with bowls of fruit, nuts and other snacks plus all kinds of drinks, and almost your own personal stewardess. It could easily spoil a person.

Normandy, 2003

In 1984 I was in Italy with SPAN students, (as I indicated in an earlier chapter), and I had a good deal of time to do my own work (mostly reading and research). I spent about a month in Rome and a month in Florence. In Florence I decided to take a course in Italian in an attempt to improve my command of that beautiful language. The class consisted mostly of college kids, but there was one French lady, Françoise Alptoona Riviere, who was close to my age. She was a librarian from Paris. We became friends and talked during the breaks. When Mary Ann and I began stopping in Paris on our way to and from Avignon, I decided to get back in touch with Françoise. Luckily the library she worked in was very close to our hotel, the Hotel des Balcons, a favorite of Macalester faculty members. It was close to the Left Bank and to the Sorbonne where we had many pleasant visits with Françoise. In 2003 she offered to let us stay at the condo she and her brother owned in Cabourg, Normandy. It is a small place, but perfect for people who like to swim in the sea or just want a place to sleep. For us it served as a home base from which to explore Normandy.

Each day we would drive in our rented car to such places as Deauville and Trouville, art colonies and two of the most charming places in France or in the world for that matter. Mont San Michele is a Benedictine abbey that sits on top of a rocky islet one mile from the coast. Visiting it was an unforgettable religious, aesthetic and historical experience. We also visited the D-Day landings sites and the cemeteries where thousands of GIs who gave their lives fighting to defeat the Nazis are buried. It is one of the saddest places I've ever visited, and it drives home forcefully the stupidity of war and yet its occasional necessity. The people of this part of France, by the way, remember what the U.S. did to free their country. There is very little anti-Americanism in Normandy which can't be said of other parts of

France. We also visited the war museum in Caen, one of the best museums of that sort of the world, and we made a special trip to Rouen to visit the cathedral which unfortunately was closed for restorations. We resolved to return to Normandy which we did, in fact, the following summer.

That time, though, we spent a week in Brittany where we made Saint-Malo our base for explorations of the province. Brittany is most famous for its megaliths which date from the Neolithic Age. The largest collection is near Carnac where they are lined up for miles. No one has ever figured out what the purpose of these huge stones was; they are every bit as mysterious as Stonehenge. Also of interest to me, at least, is the Breton language which is still spoken by approximately 200,000 people in that part of France. Breton is a Celtic language related to Cornish and Welsh. Needless to say, it is an endangered language since very few young people are learning it.

Romania, 2005

In 2005 we decided to visit Romania. We had never visited a former East Block country; the dollar was weak in Western Europe, and it seemed like the time to go there. At conferences in Greece we had met Dr. Savulescu, a homeopathic physician and philosopher and his wife Corrina. As is our custom, we wrote them saying we would be in Bucharest for a few days and asked if they'd like to meet us for lunch sometime. Much to our surprise "Geo," as we came to know him, responded immediately, and said he wanted to drive us around the country for six days. Mary Ann's reaction was "It's either going to be wonderful or terrible." Fortunately it was wonderful and even better. While at the conferences in Greece, Geo had appeared to be somewhat stiff and formal, in his homeland he was a "jolly good fellow" with a great sense of humor, a very kind heart, and a world of knowledge and experience.

We flew to Bucharest on an antique turbojet of the sort Olympic Airways uses to fly to the Aegean islands. Although I wasn't sure the plane would make it over the mountains, it did, and we arrived at the Bucharest airport safely although a couple of hours late. Geo and Corrina had been waiting patiently the whole time. After showing us around Bucharest for a day or so, Geo and I worked out the financing of the six-day tour, and we left in his rundown Ford Escort station wagon. It had cobwebs in the corners of the front windows, and the backseat where Mary Ann rode was covered with dog hairs. On the road Geo played Orthodox Christmas carols, the only tapes he had. Since they were not familiar to us, it wasn't as if we had to listen to Jingle Bells and Rudolph the Red Nosed Reindeer for six days.

Let me explain that Bucharest is a beautiful city laid out à la Paris with huge city squares and very wide, impressive boulevards. There are many beautiful buildings and parks, and there are museums, both indoor and outdoor ones, art galleries, and churches, all worth visiting. The biggest problem is the infrastructure which, our friends told us, the Communists had neglected. As one walks around Bucharest, it is imperative to watch the sidewalk carefully. In many places bricks are missing, and occasionally there might be a pipe or something else suddenly sticking up. Downtown one could easily fall into the basement of a store since there are stairs without railings starting on the sidewalks. In the front of our hotel, the Opera Hotel, every morning workman would dig a huge trench in the street looking for leaky pipes, I assumed; by the end of the day the hole would be filled in and the cobblestones replaced. Next day the whole process would be repeated. There is only one good highway in Romania, and it was closed because of a flood. The roads we drove on were among the worst in the world.

Geo drove us first to Sigishoara, the birthplace of Dracula, a charming city with strong Bavarian influences. From there we went to the northeast part of the country to visit the famous painted monasteries of Bucovina. Every square inch of the exterior of these structures is painted with scenes from the Bible or lives of the saints, and in one case ancient Greek philosophers who were thought to have prepared the world for the coming of Christianity.

Geo is my age and has many of the same interests and habits. Each day was planned so there would be time for a siesta, and we always had beer with supper, not wine. His favorite brand of beer was called "Dracula." We stayed in small hotels which were clean and comfortable. Even if we were on the third or fourth floor, I always took the stairs since the elevators in Romania are about four feet square and power failures were a daily occurrence.

On our busiest day we climbed two mountains where there were Roman forts that Geo wanted to see. Apparently the Romans had a problem with illegal immigrants, and they built these fortresses for their soldiers who were trying to keep the barbarians from entering through the valleys between the mountains. In each case Geo drove up the mountain as far as the car would go, and then we walked. Everything went well on the first climb. (Actually we were hiking up trails, not doing real mountain-climbing with ropes, etc. Mary Ann, in fact, was wearing a white dress and jewelry; neither of us knew exactly what we were getting into.) While we were at the top of the second mountain, Mary Ann noticed that it was raining in the distance. When we got back to the car, we discovered that the road was flooded. In fact the road down looked more like a river than a road. I had visions of spending the night in the car. We considered leaving Mary Ann in the car while Geo and I hiked down in search of help. Then Geo decided he would try driving, and we made it although at times it seemed the car was floating and other times the bottom was hitting rocks. What an adventure!

Everywhere we went, Geo, a true extrovert, talked to people—Gypsies, Hungarians, Germans, whomever we met, and he always introduced us. Many people in outlying areas had never met Americans before. One day Geo stopped for a little old lady who was hitchhiking. She must have been at least ninety, and she was going to visit her dentist whose office was about fifty kilometers away. She got into the back seat with Mary Ann and immediately began talking to her in Romanian. Geo explained that we were Americans and couldn't understand Romanian. She exclaimed, "Americans, Americans, AMERICANS!" Geo explained that at the end of World War II, when the Nazis retreated, many Romanians said, "Now the English and the Americans will come and everything will be fine." Instead the damned Russians moved in, and decades of Communist control followed. Ceaucescu, a brutal dictator came to power in 1965. On Christmas day 1989 he and his wife were executed by a firing squad after a military tribunal found them guilty of genocide, crimes against the state, and other charges. Crowds poured into the streets to dance and celebrate. We toured the parts of Ceausescu's palace that are open to the public. It is said to be the second largest building in the world (the largest being the Pentagon) with its 1,000 rooms, 4,500 chandeliers, huge marble columns, gold-leaf decorations, and a ballroom with a skylight large enough to accommodate a helicopter, according to our guide. Today the parliament meets there, and it is called the Palace of the People. To clear land for what the people then called the Madman's Palace 7,000 homes and twenty-six churches were demolished. Today packs of wild dogs wander the streets of Bucharest, descendents of dogs turned out when their masters' houses were destroyed.

In the northern part of the country we saw as many horse-drawn wagons as cars. Families, going to town in wagons, held blue plastic tarps over their heads when it rained. Most of the cars we saw were older, and we were told that the Germans send to Romania used cars that no one in Germany wants. We also saw families in the fields cutting grain with scythes. They used pitchforks to place the cut grain on racks where it was left to dry. In Bucharest too we saw men cutting grass and weeds with scythes, not lawnmowers.

Back in Bucharest Corinna served us dinner in their spacious backyard. She is a novelist and the author of four or five "best-sellers," none of which has been translated into English. She also gave us a tour of their house and showed us her library that consisted of two thousand (or it may have been four thousand) volumes and was located in the living room. One thing we didn't see was a kitchen, and we concluded that it may have been in a separate little building that was located in the backyard.

I have rambled on about Romania at greater length than is my wont since it was one of our very best vacations, thanks in large part to our friends the Savulescus. As so often happened, we departed thanking God for the freedom, prosperity, opportunities and everything else we enjoy as Americans.

Vienna and Berlin, 2006

In 2006, finally following our plan to go to a city, settled down for a week, and visit the sites leisurely, we decided to spend a week in Vienna and week in Berlin. Two thousand and six happened to be the 250th anniversary of Mozart's birth. Hence Vienna was even more magical than usual. Everywhere in the central part of city there were men dressed as Mozart, mimes, musicians, and hucksters. There was music everywhere, and not just the usual violinists, harpists, and saxophone players; there were quartets, sextets, singers, and one pianist who had put wheels on her piano and located it in the middle of the pedestrian mall.

Friends had recommended a small hotel about one block from Stephansdom, the Cathedral of St. Stephen, which dominates the very heart of Vienna. From our hotel we were able to walk to most of the important sites. If what we wanted to see was too far to walk to, we used public transportation. As in most great cities today, one can get an overview of the city by hopping a ride on certain trams, getting on and off at will. I recall only one taxi ride, and that was after an opera when, in our opinion, it was too late to go about on foot. On our first full day in Vienna we visited the Hofburg, the former royal palace, that now houses several museums. We succeeded in visiting three of them, and discovered that that was too many.

It's much easier (and better for a person) to walk around than to stand in one place for a long time as one can do in an art gallery or museum. Exhausted by our visit, we resolve never to attempt three museums in one day again. Other Viennese attractions included the Belvedere and its superb collection of paintings by Gustav Klimt, a favorite of Mary Ann's, the Schonbrunn, the summer residence of the Habsburgs, complete with gardens, woods, fountains, and a zoo. The Freud Museum and Wittgenstein's house had special meaning to us for different reasons. As is our practice wherever we go, we spent a good deal of time walking through outdoor markets, sitting at sidewalk cafés, reading guidebooks, people watching, and sampling the local cuisine. At the end of the week we left for Berlin knowing that we had barely scratched the surface of Vienna.

Our visit to Berlin was greatly enhanced thanks to Dirk Verheyen, a former student. Dirk grew up in the Netherlands where he attended a classical gymnasium, one of those schools where students study Latin for six years and Greek for five years before they go to college. He came to Macalester years ahead of other students in our department, and easily finished majors in classics and international studies. After earning a Ph.D. in political science at Berkeley, he taught in the United States for fifteen years before accepting the directorship of an institute in Berlin that offers courses for students from other countries. I contacted Dirk before we left home, and he very kindly recommended a small hotel located just around the corner from his condo in a green, cool, and leafy suburb.

By chance Dirk was leading a group of students on his well-known Berlin Wall walk on our first full day there. He let us join the group and provided us with earphones so we can follow his lecture which was in English. It was a wonderful introduction to Berlin and a marvelous review of history from the end of World War II to the present, including the building of the wall and its demolition in 1989. Although there were students from former East Bloc countries in the group, Dirk did not mince words regarding the "criminal dictatorship of East Germany," and the various Communist regimes. One thing was absolutely clear: the people of Berlin despised the wall intensely, and they are still furious about it.

When Dirk discussed the Berlin airlift (June 1948 to May 1949), which was necessitated by the Soviet blockade of railroads and highways from the west into Berlin, he pointed out that the United States, England, and some Commonwealth nations made 200,000 flights bringing 13,000 tons of food and other supplies daily. In answer to my question regarding why the French didn't participate since there was a French zone along with the American and English zones, he reminded us that at the end of World War II the French had no airplanes and later they only had the used ones that the United States gave to them. When the Soviets saw that the airlift was succeeding, they gave up in humiliation. You can be sure that there is very little anti-Americanism in Berlin today.

Berlin is the site of some of the most spectacular modern architecture in the world. What strikes the visitor is the creative use of glass. This Dirk explained as the contemporary Berliners desire for transparency in contrast to the secrecy that shrouded everything the Nazis did, and one might say the Communists too.

Visiting museums in Berlin is facilitated by the fact that there are five world-class museums located on what is called Museum Island. The one that stands out in my memory is the Pergamum Museum which has three great collections: one of classical antiquities, one of near Eastern antiquities, and a museum of Islamic art. The second one has the Altar of Zeus taken from Pergamum to Berlin by the Germans in 1878. We had visited the site of Pergamum in Turkey some years earlier so this had a special meaning for us. The other museum I must mention is the new German Historical Museum which covers 2000 years of German history. It is ingeniously laid out in a large square building that has a central courtyard. One goes around from historical period to historical period. For example, "Early Cultures and the Medieval Period," "Reformation and the Thirty Years War," etc. up to the "Nazi Period And World War II," and "Divided Germany and Reunification." The exhibits are set up so that the person who wants to do an in-depth examination of any period, simply moves further back into the that area. The whole museum is a tribute to Teutonic cleverness and thoroughness.

Of course we visited the Brandenburg gate, the Charlottenburg Palace, the Reichstat, the Jewish Museum and Checkpoint Charlie. Dirk's wife served a delicious dinner on one evening, and we had a chance to get acquainted with their two beautiful children. Other evenings we sampled German fare in neighborhood restaurants, and of course, we felt obliged to taste as many of the famous German beers as possible. All in all it was a wonderful visit.

Budapest and Prague, 2007

When I arrived in Italy in 1956, I had never seen a protest or demonstration, not even on TV since we didn't have TV at home before

1958. One day friends and I were walking near the Piazza Venezia in downtown Rome when we came upon a protest. Hundreds or thousands of Italians were protesting the brutal suppression of Hungary by the Soviets. I had never seen anything like it—banners, signs, shouting, chanting, speakers, etc. Suddenly the Italian riot police arrived riding in jeeps. They drove straight into the crowd causing protesters to scatter lest they be run over, and then the police began spraying yellow dye from fire hoses mounted on the backs of the jeeps. Although most Italians sympathized with the Hungarians, the police clearly saw this protest as illegal. Later in the day people with yellow dye on them were arrested. We followed the progress of the Hungarian rebellion against the Soviets carefully, and by the end of October it appeared that the Hungarians had won with Molotov cocktails and bricks against Soviet tanks. Life began to return to normal in Budapest. The Soviets had offered to negotiate but then reneged and sent in tanks and a huge army on November 4. By November 10 Hungarian resistance had ceased. Two hundred thousand Hungarians fled their country, thousands had been killed, and Budapest was devastated. Russian dominance lasted until 1989. In 1957 I read Michener's *The Bridge at Andau,* one of his earliest novels and, in my opinion, one of his best. In 2006 I reread it in preparation for our trip. All of this helped us understand and appreciate Hungary when we visited Budapest in 2007.

Since Macalester has always stressed "internationalism" (we have students from approximately seventy-five countries; most of our American students study abroad, and we have an International Center and most recently an Institute for Global Citizenship), we have contacts all over the world. The director of our International Center put us in touch with a very charming young Hungarian lady who took a whole off day off from work to show us around Budapest. We learned from her what life is like today in Hungary and what we should do on the other days we were there.

There is evidence that the site of Budapest was inhabited as early as 2000 B.C. The Romans arrived in the first century B.C. and made it their capital of the province Panonia. Budapest *per se,* however, has only existed since 1873 and resulted from the unification of three cities Buda, Pest, and Obuda. Obuda merged with Buda and is on the west bank of the Danube, and Pest is on the east bank. Today ruins of the Roman city include viaducts, baths, villas, and a well preserved amphitheater which we visited. The modern city which has been completely rebuilt is considered one of the most beautiful cities in Europe (according to the official Hungarian tourist bureau). We were not disappointed. After visiting the Royal

Palace, the National Gallery, and several churches, we stumbled upon a fair on the famous Chain Bridge one day which gave us a chance to taste various Hungarian delicacies. Finally we soaked in the famous thermal baths, something everyone who visits Budapest should do. After a week in Budapest, our next stop was Prague. The train ride to Prague was doubly pleasant since we had a whole first class compartment to ourselves.

According to various guidebooks of Czechoslovakia, Prague comes from a Slavic word that means "ford." Hence Prague like Rome and Paris grew up at a place where it was easy to cross the river, in this case the Vitava River. All three cities also have an island in their river (it's easier to build two short bridges than one long one.)

We stayed in the Blue Rose Hotel, a moderately priced hotel with extra-large rooms and an excellent location—within a walking distance of many of the chief attractions of the city, for instance Old Town with its beautiful square and clock tower, the Charles Bridge (musicians everywhere), Wenceslaus Square (actually a huge rectangle several blocks long with shops and restaurants of both sides), and the old Jewish Cemetery. Across the river there is Prague Castle, said to be the largest castle in the world, and St. Vitus Cathedral. One half block from our hotel was the Opera House where Mozart's "Don Giovanni" was first performed.

We took two walking tours of Prague, as we had done in Paris and elsewhere. There is no better way to see a city. One of the Prague walks was especially memorable. There was only one other couple in the group, a married couple from California, and the wife turned out to be a Macalester alumna. Our guide had just received his doctorate in history from Charles University and was especially interested in architecture. In one square he pointed out examples of classical, medieval, gothic, baroque, renaissance, and modern architectural styles. (Sometimes more than one of these styles was present in one building.) There are even cubist buildings in Prague with a style borrowed from cubist painters such as Picasso and Braque. Our guide spent twice as long as usual with us since it was obvious that we were all very interested in architecture and history. Hence we thanked him with an unusually generous tip.

We spent a charming evening with the son of a friend from St. Thomas. He was studying in Prague and planned to specialize in East European history. We took him to dinner at his favorite restaurant which turned out to be not Czech but Georgian. It was our first experience with Georgian cuisine; the best thing about it is that it is inexpensive. He gave us a good idea of what student life is like in Prague. His mother had visited him recently, and Mary Ann asked what she had bought, hoping I think for tips regarding Bohemian crystal. He replied that she had bought him a new pair of sneakers and that was it! Bohemia, by the way, today refers to a region that comprises two thirds of the Czech Republic. Our historian/guide explained that the people of Czechoslovakia had never had a particularly sybaritic lifestyle. It was, according to him, Gypsies from Bohemia who went to Paris and gave "bohemian" its current connotation.

We left Prague with very happy memories. Many visitors to former East Block countries that were under Soviet rule for so long expect to find life there dull and drab. This is definitely not the case with Prague. It is a beautiful, cheerful, exciting place full of music, beautiful architecture, delicious food and friendly people. It deserves its nicknames, the "Golden City" and "the city with a hundred spires."

Other Travels

Long before I joined the Macalester faculty in 1968 the College had an "Interim Term," that is a one-month January term during which faculty members taught one course and students took one course. The teaching load in our department was three courses one semester, two courses the other semester plus one course during the January term. I believe that most senior faculty members liked the Interim Term. For one thing it gave us a chance to teach subjects we ordinarily would not have been able to teach, and it was a time to try out a new course which might later become a part of the regular curriculum. Younger faculty members, on the other hand, tended not to like having to teach a course in January. They claimed, and they were right, that more was being demanded of them for tenure and promotion especially as far as publications were concerned. They claimed that they needed January for research and writing, and so in 1996 they mustered enough votes to abolish the Interim Term. They also persuaded the president and a majority of the faculty that the course load for the two semesters should remain the same. Hence, for instance, in our department we would teach three courses one semester and two the other, and we would not be required to do anything from mid-December until the first week of February. I told Mary Ann that I wanted to go some place where it was warm and there was a good library.

In 1998, 1999, and 2000 we went to Avignon, a beautiful city in Provence. Friends in our French Department had connections at the University of Avignon and arranged for me to get library privileges, etc. On weekends we would rent a car and visit neighboring towns, many of which are famous in literature and song. We also visited Nice, Monte Carlo, and Cannes which were a little farther away. One of the best features of this plan was that it enabled us to spend a few days in Paris both going and coming. The only problem was that the second year it was quite chilly, and there is a wind, the Mistral, which blows southward down the valley of the Rhone and which was occasionally violent enough to blow trees down.

Hence we decided to try Hawaii. A friend suggested applying to the East West Center in Honolulu. I had always assumed that it was for experts in East/West relations, but it turned out that anyone from a non-profit organization could apply to stay there. Since it is subsidized by the U.S. government, rent was extremely low. Also it is located immediately across the street from the campus of the University of Hawaii and the main library. I got a lot of work done there, and Mary Ann did a good many sketches and drawings. Again on weekends we rented a car to explore the island, and a couple of times we flew to other islands. Of course, the weather was perfect. Each morning the radio announcer would say, "Good morning. It's another beautiful day in paradise!" I will be criticized for saying this, but I found Hawaii boring. After one has seen the Hula dancers, the volcanoes, the wild orchids, and a few other things, there isn't much to do. Even though we made some wonderful friends who entertained us (I think they were glad to see someone from the "mainland"), after the second year we decided to try somewhere else. I suggested the University of Texas at Austin which has a famous Classics Department and an excellent library. We only lasted one January there since it can be cool and rainy during the winter months. Finally we discovered Tuscon and the University of Arizona which has not disappointed us in any way. Contacts in the Classics Department got me "visiting scholar" status which provides me with a faculty card, parking privileges, library privileges, etc. So far we have spent six Januaries there, and, God willing, we will return again next winter.

In Holy Land, Shannon, Mary Ann and Jerry, 1993

New Year's Eve, Paris, 1998 with Francoise Alptuna Riviere

Mary Ann and Jerry, Egypt, 1999

At Great Wall, China, 2002

With friends in South Africa, 2000

CHAPTER XIII

WORD BETHUMPT

" . . . not a word of his
but buffets better than a fist of France;
Zounds, I was never so bethumpt with words
Since I first call'd my brother's father dad."

Shakespeare, "As You Like It"

I am a wordstruck, word bethumpted
word besotted, wordaholic,
unrepentant verbivore.

Richard Lederer

In a wonderful column that appeared some years ago in the *Saturday Review* the poet John Ciardi related a number of experiences he had while teaching composition after World War II. Among his students was a navy veteran who had served aboard a tanker that refueled ships at sea and whose ambition was to become a writer. In a story about his war experiences this veteran wrote, "We had arrived at our mid-ocean rendezvous." In a conference Ciardi pointed out that "arrive" comes, via French, from Latin *ripa*, "bank," "shore" *(cf.* riparian and riviera) and that the student had said in effect, "We had come to shore in mid-ocean." Did he want to say that? "Everyone knows that "to arrive" mean 'to get there' and who cares about dead Latin roots?" was his response. That student never published a thing, according to Ciardi, because he lacked the desire to engage language at a depth beyond the superficial, a desire that a good writer must have. The same student saw nothing unusual about the phrase "a crusading Egyptian social worker" even after Ciardi pointed out the derivation of crusade (Latin *crux*, "cross") and the fact that "Egyptians were not generally motivated in that direction, that they had tended, in fact, to be on the other side of those expeditions we call the crusades . . ." I believe it was Ciardi who, on another occasion, objected to the phrase "a delapidated wooden shack" on the grounds that stones (*lapides* in Latin) don't fall off wooden shacks. He likewise found fault with "supercilious wave of the hand" because it involved a comic confusion of anatomy (*supercilium* is Latin for eyebrow). I heard Ciardi speak once in St. Paul, and he confessed that he was a "compulsive etymologizer." He was the first person I had met who suffered from the same strange affliction I suffered from for about thirty years, i.e. a compulsion to trace the etymology of every word I encountered. I came to feel that I didn't really know a word unless I knew its origin—Latin, Greek, Anglo-Saxon, or whatever and better yet its Proto-Indo-European root. I hope readers will discover, as I did, that this is actually a blessing and the source of many insights and much joy. In my case this fascination with the origins of words seems to have begun with two courses I was asked to teach at the U. of South Dakota—"Scientific Terminology" and "Derivatives." In this chapter I want to share with readers some of the fruits of my passion for etymology and perhaps even engender it in others.

A friend attended a seminar on "thanatology" (on death and dying). She said they discussed death as a" viable alternative!" Besides using a dreadful cliche, she had come close to saying that death is a live option since viable comes through French *vie* from Latin *vita* and means "capable of living." Had it been deliberate, I might have been impressed by her use of oxymoron. I am reminded of the police chief who called charges of graft in his department "potentially factual" and of the corporation executive who said that the accident at Three Mile Island was a "normal aberration."

W. H. Auden, another poet, was once asked what advice he would give an aspiring poet. Auden said he would ask why the person wanted to write. "If the answer was 'Because I have something terribly important to say' . . . there could be small hope of expecting poetry from him. If, on the other hand, the answer was 'Because I like to hang around words and overhear them whisper to one another,' then that man might fail of any of thousands of human reasons, but he had a poet's interest in the poem and could be hoped for."

A by-product of the study of Latin and a goal of the study of "derivatives" should be not only a numerical increase in the size of the students' vocabularies, but the enhancement of their ability to appreciate the deeper levels of meanings words have. I always tried to make my students philologists in the etymological sense of the word (lovers of words and language) and share with them the joy that comes from "hanging around words." Now, there may be people who have developed a love for words and an appreciation for their histories and connotations without studying Latin, but they are indeed *rarae aves*. Clearly the study of Latin is the best way to become a connoisseur of words, and clearly vocabulary building courses are "second best." Nevertheless, given the difficulty (often impossibility) of requiring or persuading students to take Latin, courses that deal with roots, prefixes, suffixes, word-formation, etymology, etc. suddenly seem very important.

Charles Ferguson, senior editor emeritus of *Reader's Digest*, novelist, biographer *(Naked to Mine Enemies)*, essayist, lecturer, historian *(Organizing to Beat The Devil*, a history of the Methodist Church), teacher *(Say It with Words)* and logophile extrordinaire used to visit Macalester every year, and we became friends. He once wrote in a letter to me that a word "should be treated as an entity, as an Emersonian person so real it will bleed, as a world that sums up eons of life, as a thing in itself, not a blob on a page or a noise in the ear. A word is to be seen as history marvelously compressed, as a distillate of human experience because it has had human experience passing in and out of minds and across tongues in countless situations, witnessing and savoring what has gone on in *its* presence and by means of it." Mr. Ferguson reminds us of Samuel Coleridge's statement that "there are cases in which more knowledge of more value may be expressed by the history of a word than by the history of a campaign." Thanks to the generosity of "Fergy," as we called him, Macalester had for a number of years a "Word Library," a special room in the library with a collection of dictionaries, lexicons, and books about words, of which there is a surprising number. It was Fergy's ambition to make it "the best known and most used bank of word data in the world" and to make Macalester a center for the study of words (not of linguistics or semantics or of any -ology, but of plain old words." After Mr. Ferguson's death and the construction of the new library, the "Word Library" unfortunately ceased to exist.

Words come with retinues of associations and connotations. They have textures, shapes, tastes and histories. Words have their particular demands upon the speech muscles. According to George Steiner words have "angularities," "concavities," "forces of tectonic suggestion," and "rugosity" (wrinkles); for poets words even have distinctive smells. Homer speaks of "wooly" screams, Dante of "hairy" and "shaggy"' words, also "combed out," "glossy," and "rumpled" ones. Pablo Neruda, the Chilean writer, says, "Words have shadow, transparence, weight, feathers, hair, and everything gathered from so much wandering from country to country, from being

roots so long . . . Words are very ancient and very new . . . ." And again
"I run after certain words . . . they are so beautiful that I want to fit them
all into my poem . . . I catch them in midflight, as they buzz past, I trap
them, clean them, peel them, I set myself in front of the dish, they have a
crystalline texture to me, vibrant, ivory, vegetable, oily, like fruit, like algae,
like agates, like olives. And then I stir them, I shake them, I drink them,
I gulp them down, I mash them, I garnish them, I let them go . . . I leave
them in my poem like stalactites, like slivers of polished wood, like coals,
pickings from a shipwreck, gifts from the waves . . . Everything exists in
the word."

Beside poets no one is more sensitive to these dimensions of language
today than Madison Avenue. "There are tall, skinny words and short, fat
ones, and strong ones and weak ones, and boy words and girl words," writes
an advertising agency. Fire, passion, explode, smash and attack are described
as red words. Moss, brook, cool, solitude and hammock are examples of
green words. There are also black words (funeral, tomb, somber) and beige
ones (abstruse, clerk, and float). "Shout is red, persuade is green, rave is
black and listen is beige." Young words are pancake, bat, ball and surprise;
old ones, Packard, lavender and velvet. "Confident, smug words" are proud,
stare, dare and major; ulcer, itch and stomach are worried words. "Joe is
confident; Horace is worried." Some words are round, some oblong, some
are shaped like Rorschach ink blots, some are square. There are fast words
and slow words too. "Wilkinsburg, as you would expect, is dry, square, old
and light gray." Truly, as Emerson said, "language is fossil poetry."

Words can be important source of insight, and there have been
philosophers who showed great interest in the ancient wisdom enshrined in
them. William Barrett says this about the German philosopher Heidegger:
"The etymologies of words, particularly Greek words are a passion with
Heidegger; in his pursuit of them he has been accused of playing with
words, but when one realizes what deposits of truth mankind has let slip
into its language as it evolves, Heidegger's perpetual digging at words to
get at their hidden nuggets of meaning is one of his most exciting facets.
In the matter of Greek particularly—a dead language whose whole history
is now spread out before us—we can see how certain truths are embedded
in the language itself; truths that the Greek race later came to *forget* in
its thinking. The word 'phenomenon'—a word in ordinary usage, by this
time, in all modern European languages—means in Greek 'that which
reveals itself.' Phenomenology therefore means for Heidegger the attempt
to let the thing speak for itself. Heidegger finds around that word a whole

cluster of etymologies, all of them having an internal unity of meaning that brings us to the very center of his thought. The etymology of the Greek word for truth, *aletheia*, is another key to Heidegger's theory: the word means literally, "unhiddenness," "revelation." Truth occurs when what has been hidden is no longer so." Finally, "It is by harking back to the primeval meaning of truth as it became embedded in the Greek language that Heidegger takes his theory in a single leap beyond the boundaries of Husserl's phenomenology."

William James in a chapter on mysticism in *Varieties of Religious Experience* discusses the insights that individual words or phrases can produce. These insights are the "simplest rudiment of mystical experience. They lie at one extreme of a continuum, the end that usually makes no claims regarding supernatural origin or content. An author named John Foster testified that "single words (as *chalcedony*), or the names of ancient heroes, had a mighty fascination over him. 'At any time the word hermit was enough to transport him.' The words *woods* and *forest* would produce the most powerful emotion." A German lady confessed to James that "Philadelphia" had haunted her all her life, and she longed to visit the city that had such a wondrous name. Martin Luther one day when be heard a fellow monk recite the words from the creed, "I believe in the forgiveness of sins" says he suddenly saw the scriptures in a new light; he felt as if he had been born again. It was as if "I had found the door of Paradise thrown wide open."

It is well known that the name *Oedipus* can mean etymologically "know foot" and "swell-foot." John Hay, author of a recent book on *Oedipus the King,* believes that the "catalytic insight," the "epiphany" (defined as "the sudden realization of the *whatness* of a thing") that made the greatest of tragedies possible came to Sophocles as he contemplated the possible meanings of Oedipus' name. Sophocles did not take one meaning and reject the other; he considered both meanings simultaneously and saw that lameness was an apt metaphor for human knowledge. Human knowing is like the journey of a lame man! Sophocles calls the audience's attention to this insight by means of etymological wordplay, which, Hay says, is a "major source of insight and irony. It goes back to the root-meanings of the word for a fresh or 'reborn' slant."

Margaret Schlauch has an admirable discussion of the etymological use of words by poets in Chapter 9 of *The Gift of Language* where she gives a number of excellent examples. Her conclusion: "Sophisticated writers still impose the etymological task upon their readers as part of the aesthetic experience. It may be said, in fact, that etymology is one of the devices by which readers are now called upon to share in the creative act."

The remainder of this chapter provides examples of curiosities and oddities and even some non-trivial matters which readers may find of interest. I used to use these for three or four minutes at the beginning of classes to capture the students' attention and to inject a bit of levity into the learning process. Also, when Macalester had a one-month January term, I taught a course called "Philology for Logophiles" a couple of times which was designed to interest students in Latin, Greek, and linguistics. A whole course in "recreational linguistics" was offered at the University of Massachusetts, Amherst which dealt exclusively with word games, puzzles, euphemisms, limericks, double dactyls, macaronic verse, word squares, *etc.*

The literary avant-garde: There used to be in Paris a group of writers and intellectuals who call themselves "Oulipo," short for *Ouvroir de Letterature Potentielle* ("Workshop of Potential Literature"). They met monthly to discuss experimental forms. An American member invented "perverbs" (perverted proverbs), *e.g.* "Think twice before speaking to a friend in need." Another member composed the longest known palindrome, a 5,000 word treatise on palindromes. Another composed *Cent Mille Milliards de Poems (A Hundred Thousand Billion Poems).* The reader can construct 10^{14} intelligible sonnets by flipping strips of paper each of which contains one verse. Other fruits of their labors include Spoonerisms, poems on Mobius strips and emblematic poems (poems shaped like pyramids, hearts, bottles, *etc.).*

Lipograms are compositions that leave out one letter of the alphabet. Georges Perec, a contemporary French novelist, for instance, wrote a "highly praised novel," *La Disparition,* in which there is not a single e. (Some critics didn't notice the omission!) Ernest V. Wright likewise used no e's in his 50,000 word novel *Gadsby;* he tied the E type-bar down in his typewriter. (For a discussion of the difficulties involved in such an effort see Martin Gardiner's note in *Oddities and Curiosities of Words and Literature* by C. Bombaugh. Gardiner does not, unfortunately, tell us why people write lipograms.) Pindar, the ancient Greek poet, according to Athenaeus, wrote an ode without sigmas, and according to Addison (#50 of the *Spectator)* one Tryphiodorus wrote an *Odyssey* in 24 books ostracizing alpha from the first book, beta from the second, etc.

At the other end of the spectrum, a monk named Hucbald used only words beginning with c in his *Ecloga de Laudibus Calvitti (Carmina clarisonae calvis cantate Camenae/ comere condigno conabor carmine caivas. etc.)* There is also the *Pugna Porcorum* by Petrus Placentius in which every word begins with, guess what.

Palindromes: (Spelled the same forwards and backwards) "Eva, can I pose as Aesop in a cave?" "Red rum, sir, is murder." There are hundreds more of these in Howard W. Bergerson's *Palindromes and Anagrams;* Bombaugh also has a short chapter on palindromes which includes several in Latin and Greek (Lawyer's motto: Si *nummi, immunis.* "If you have money, you're immune.") According to an article in the N.Y. Times, *Roma, summus amor* was found among the graffiti on the walls of a tavern recently by archaeologists excavating under *Santa Maria Maggiore* in Rome. If one wants more palindromes, see "Manner of Speaking" by J. Ciardi for more example and further bibliography or contact Professor Otto R. Osseforp, % *The Wall Street Journal.*

Centos (Latin, "a garment made of rags sewed together, a patchwork ") are poems that consist of lines and phrases taken from other poems; they are also called "mosaic poems." The *Cento Nuptialis* of Ausonius is perhaps the most famous example. The Empress Eudoxia wrote a life of Christ using lines and parts of lines from Homer, and Proba Falconia and Alexander Ross *(fl. 1769)* did the same using Vergil. There are modern examples in Bombaugh.

Anagrams (=Ars Magna) a "frivolous and now almost obsolete intellectual exercise" according to Bombaugh. The letters of the first line should be rearranged to form a second line which must say something relevant to the first, *e.g.* James Stuart—A just master. Imperators/A prime sort. Senator/A Nestor. Sinecure/Sure nice! *Supremus Pontifex Romanus/O non sum super petram fixus.* United States/*In te Deus stat.*

Neologisms: Gelett Burgess once wrote a dictionary containing several hundred words he had coined, entitled *Burgess Unabridged. A Dictionary of Words You Have Always Needed.* As far as I know only two of his coinages have made it into other dictionaries, "goop" and "blurb." Other examples: "Lallifaction, n. A verbose story, a joke repeated" and "Huzzlecoo, n. 1. An intimate talk; a 'heart-to-heart talk,' a conversation. 2. A flirtation." The editor of the *National Observer* coined some new words and was deluged with readers' own inventions. Among the better ones: "Xerocracy, government by photocopy." "Idiolectuals, overschooled and undereducated nitwits who have solutions for all problems." and "Msdemeanor, any offense against women's liberation." "Factoid" was coined by Norman Mailer. Coining words would be a good exercise for students and could even teach them something about word formation. One might start with new names for groups a la "pride of lions," "parliament of owls," and "nide of pheasants," *e.g"* a "declension of Latin teachers."

Improper nouns: What do silhouette, zeppelin, raglan, cardigan, leotard, tawdry and dunce have in common? The same thing that ocean, pamphlet, joviality, martial and kewpie share—they were once all proper nouns, i.e. people's names. There are eighty-two of these in *Word People* by Nancy Sorel and hundreds, perhaps thousands, in Willard Espy's *Thou Improper, Thou Uncommon Noun.*

Rare words: Mrs. Byrne's *Dictionary of Unusual, Obscure and Preposterous Words* is guaranteed to provide hours of enjoyment for logophiles. There one learns what a *fossarian* is, also what *clinomania* is and what *luctiferous, apopemploclinic; cinerescent* and *retromingent* mean. *Poplollies and Bellibones* have more of the same: *blore, faffle, iswonk, keak, quop* and *snollygoster* are examples. Students are amused by words such as *nosarian* (one who believes that there is no limit to the possible size of noses). They should, however, be warned not to waste time learning them, although such "nonce words" could be used to test students' knowledge of constituent elements.

More Perverbs: "When in Rome, do it yourself." "Two heads are better than none." "Don't count your chickens in midstream." "No news is the mother of invention." "A fool and his money is a friend indeed."

Redundancies: Rules and regulations, due and payable, hoot and holler, leaps and bounds, neat and tidy, vim and vigor, tattered and torn, plain and simple, rant and rave, aches and pains, cease and desist, null and void, over and above, lord and master, each and every, prim and proper, safe and sound, and there are many more. Some of these are legal phrases.

Malaproprisms: "She has really plummeted to the top." "He's going up and down like a metronome." "Republicans understand the importance of bondage between a mother and child." (Dan Quayle) "Well, that was a cliff-dweller." (Re a close game.) "We seem to have unleased a hornet's nest." "He's as headstrong as an allegory on the banks of the Nile." (Mrs. Malaprop herself).

Aptonyms: (a hideous hybrid word since "apt-" is Latin and "-onym" is Greek, but you'll get the idea.) Cardinal Sin was the head of the Catholic Church in the Philippines. Mr. Sues is a lawyer. Miss Cashdollar was the treasurer of a school. Linda Toot played the flute in the Milwaukee Symphony. John Wisdom is an American philosopher. Dr. Richard Bone is an osteopath. A guy named Hooker runs a bait shop. Dr. I. Doctor, Eye Doctor, is an ophthalmologist. There's a used car dealer named Karl Krook. Jared Wooley raises sheep. Dr. Hertz was a dentist in Ft. Lauderdale, Dr. Slaughter is an oral surgeon, Dr. Coffin, M.D. is a general practitioner! and Rev. D. Goodenough is a Methodist minister.

Linguicide: "Did I hear you say 'hopefullywise'?" (cartoon) "Dvorak was a late bloomer compositionwise." (Program notes) "She was as pure as a vestigial virgin:' (student paper) "He was a life long native of N. Y." (N. Y. Times). "We must tentify these conclusions." (bureaucrat) "Young juvenilcs" (mayor of Boston) "a false lie" (Billy Martin) "free gifts" (bank: ad), focalize, prioritize. youthfulize, deniability and on and on. Pomposity, redundancy, evasiveness, ambiguity, obfuscation, jargon and psychobabble everywhere, but the question is, "Is it serious?" Yes, according to Richard Mitchell, "The Undergound Grammarian, who makes a very strong case for traditional ideas about grammar and composition in *Less Than Words Can Say.* The classic discussion of this subject, however, is George Orwell's essay, "Politics and the English Language." He thought it was a serious matter: "But if thought corrupts language, language can also corrupt thought." According to Sydney J. Harris, the columnist, "If the level of verbal expression is low, the only other form of expression is physical." In other words, those who are unable to express themselves verbally are more likely to resort to the fist (or a gun) than those who are articulate. Without an adequate vocabulary "such abstract ideas as justice, honesty, personal property, law, courtesy and thoughtfulness for others seem impossible to comprehend."

In 2004 I read an article by a high school English teacher in a local publication in which she explained that most public schools no longer teach grammar explicitly, only implicitly. I took this to mean that they don't teach it at all, which in many cases is true. She explained that teaching grammar would take time away from teaching more valuable "higher order thinking skills" such as analysis, synthesis, critical thinking and even "metacognitive strategies" (thinking about one's thinking). This article provoked me to write an op-ed piece in which I complained that many students come to college not knowing the parts of speech or even how to pick out the subject and predicate in a sentence. I told a story about coming to a chapter on participles in an elementary Latin class. I asked if anyone knew what a participle was. After a long silence a young lady said, "They are not supposed to dangle." That was the sum total of the class's knowledge of participles. She didn't know what a participle was, but she had heard that they are not supposed to dangle. I then argued in my essay that it is absurd to think that students who can't analyze a sentence will be able to analyze an argument, an editorial, or a campaign speech. *The Pioneer Press* published my piece under the title "Our Participles are Dangling and We Don't Even Know It."

A short time later the *Wall Street Journal* ran a story in which the author claimed that the public schools were doing a poor job of teaching grammar. I revised my *Pioneer Press* essay somewhat and send it to the *Journal* which published it under the title "Us Don't Need Grammar for Higher Order Thinking Skills." As a result of these efforts, I received a phone call from a gentleman who was the president of a group called the "Wordos". He wanted to come to my office to talk with me about grammar and related subjects, and, of course, I invited him to come. The Wordos are retired editors, reporters and writers who meet once a month to discuss words and grammar and language in general. Between meetings, as they read newspapers, listen to the radio, watch TV, etc. they scrutinize everything for grammatical errors, stylistic infelicities, neologisms, and other linguistic matters of interest. These are discussed at the monthly meetings, after which the president puts out a newsletter which is sent to 350 newspapers in Minnesota. When I asked what sort of replies he receives, he replied, "The silence is thunderous." The Wordos invited me to speak at their next meeting which I did, and then they invited me to join, which I also did.

At seventy I was one of the youngest members. Most are in their 80s; one resigned shortly after I joined explaining that he would soon celebrate his 90th birthday. At our meetings we have a hilarious time, and I look forward eagerly to each session. Following the format used in earlier parts of this chapter, I will share with readers some of the gems garnered at meetings of the Wordos.

Amusing headlines: "One-armed man applauds the kindness of strangers," "Statistics show that teen pregnancy drops off significantly after age 25," "Attorney accidentally sues himself," "County to pay $250,000 to advertise lack of funds," "Tiger Woods plays with own balls, Nike says," "Federal Agents Raid Gun Shop, Find Weapons," "Fish need water, Feds say." "Community rallies to help massacre survivors." "University of Akron students protest invasion by Israel." "Lawmaker questions prison costs of killing suspect." "A religious mother questions her beliefs after her gay son kills himself and eventually joins the crusade for gay rights." Coupon: "Get 50% off or half price, whichever is less."

Why English is not easy: "The farm used to produce produce." "We must polish the Polish furniture." "He could lead if he would get the lead out." "The soldier decided to desert his dessert in the desert." "Since there is no time like the present, he thought it was time to present the present." "When shot at, the dove dove into the bushes." "The buck does funny things when the does are present." "To help with planting, the farmer taught his sow to sow." "The wind was too strong to wind the sail." Note the following: "There is no egg in eggplant, nor ham in hamburger; neither apple nor pine in pineapple. French fries weren't invented in France. Sweetmeats are candies while sweetbreads, which aren't sweet, are meat. Quicksand works slowly, boxing rings are square, and a guinea pig is neither from Guinea nor is it a pig."

Things that make Wordos [sic]: Using "less" where "fewer" is called for (e.g. in supermarket, "Ten items or less." "Between you and I." "Myself" as subject ("Myself and my wife are going to the movie.") "Who" used instead of "whom." (This is a lost cause; "whom" is doomed.) Using "like" instead of "as." Using the plural pronoun to refer to one person: "Each student should bring their book." Using an adjective where an adverb is called for: "She learns very quick." Using the indicative in a contrary-to-fact condition: "If it was raining, I would be unhappy." (Should be "If it were raining . . .") Not using the possessive before a gerund (a word ending in -ing used as a noun): "Aside from him being an athlete . . ." "If you don't mind me asking . . ." "Us working together is very important . . ." (Obama) "Thusly" for "Thus" ("Thus" is an adverb and doesn't need the

"-ly.") "Hopefully" (The dog went home hopefully.) "Alright" is not all right. Confusion between "lie" and "lay" (Another lost cause, I fear.)

I conclude with this quote from a review of John Moore's *You English Words*: "If a man must go soppy about something—and no doubt a man must—what better object could there be for his daft, uncritical, wife-maddening, friend-alienating affection than the English language?" (*Time*, August, 1962).

CHAPTER XIV

MY PHILOSOPHY AND MY THEOLOGY

"It is a great advantage for a system of philosophy to be substantially true."

George Santayana

There is nothing so absurd or incredible that it has not been asserted by one philosopher or another.

Descartes

The audience I have in mind for this chapter consists of my grandchildren after they have gone to college and had a course or two in philosophy, but I sincerely hope that others will find it of interest too. I first discuss philosophy and then theology. Philosophy could be defined as a purely rational attempt to understand everything. It includes such subfields as epistemology (theory of knowledge), esthetics (the study of beauty), ethics (the study of what is morally right and wrong), ontology (what is ultimately real), theodicy (arguments for the existence of God), logic (the art or science of right reasoning), and other even more esoteric fields. Most theologians would accept St. Anslem's definition of theology as "faith seeking understanding." Philosophy thus is based on reason; theology on faith. Philosophy has been called the "handmaiden of theology" (*ancilla theologiae*) because, if one does theology systematically, one will need philosophy; i.e. one will have epistemological assumptions, ontological assumptions, logical ones, etc. While I am a professional philologist, I am an amateur philosopher, and the philosophy I have advocated in classes and am most allied with is called "realism."

Realism has been called the natural philosophy of the human mind, "*la metaphysique naturelle de l'esprit humain*," as the French philosopher

Henri Bergson put it. Recently the distinguished American philosopher John Searle dubbed it the "default position" in philosophy, that is, it is the position people hold before they study philosophy, and it is the position they fall back on in living their lives, regardless of what they may say in lectures or write in scholarly journals or books. Here, quoting Searle, are the "default" positions on some major questions:

> There is a real world that exists independently of us, independent of our experiences, our thoughts, our language.

> We have direct perceptual access to that world through our senses . . .

> Words in our language, words like rabbit or tree, typically have reasonably clear meanings. Because of their meanings, they can be used to refer to and talk about real objects in the world.

> Our statements are typically true or false, depending on whether they correspond to how things are, that is, to the facts in the world.

When one studies the history of Western philosophy, one discovers that it is an account of one -ism after another. Platonism, idealism, stoicism, Epicureanism, skepticism, cynicism, neo-Platonism, scholasticism, and so forth right up to modern movements such as logical positivism, existentialism, historicism, deconstructionism and postmodernism. All of these have sprung up, flourished for a time, perhaps made a contribution, and then faded away to become chapters or footnotes in a history of philosophy textbook. Realism, however, is the one school that has endured through the centuries. Aristotle is the father of realism, and St. Thomas Aquinas was his greatest follower and champion. Realism has, therefore, been called the "perennial philosophy." It consists of a "body of basic philosophical truths that is enduring, abiding, permanent, eternal—a philosophy that is as old and as new as philosophical speculation itself. It is one whose validity and truth is not confined to any particular age or civilization . . ." (*A Realistic Philosophy* by K. F. Reinhardt)

The perennial philosophy of Aristotle and Aquinas has been beautifully described by the French philosopher Jacques Maritain in the following passage which, although long, deserves to be quoted in full: "It is . . . the philosophy of *being*, entirely supported by and modeled upon what *is*, and scrupulously respecting every demand of reality—the philosophy of *intellect* which it trusts as the faculty which attains truth and forms by a discipline which is an incomparable mental purification. And for this very reason it proves itself the *universal* philosophy in the sense that it does not reflect a nationality, class, group, temperament, or race, the ambition or melancholy of an individual or any practical need, but is the expression and product of *reason which is everywhere the same*; and in this sense also, that it is capable of leading the finest intellects to the most sublime knowledge and the most difficult of attainment, yet without once betraying those vital convictions, instinctively required by every same mind, which compose the domain, wide as humanity, of common sense. It can therefore claim to be abiding and permanent (*philosophia perennis*) in the sense that before Aristotle and St. Thomas had given it scientific formulation as a systematic philosophy, it existed from the dawn of humanity in germ and in the prephilosophic state, as an instinct of the understanding and a natural knowledge of the first principles of reason and ever since its foundation as a system has remained firm and progressive, a powerful and living tradition, while all other philosophies have been born and have died in turn. And, finally, it stands out as being . . . one; one because it alone bestows harmony and unity on human knowledge, both philosophical and scientific, and one because in itself it realizes a maximum of consistency in a maximum of complexity, and neglect to the least of its principles involves the most unexpected consequences, distorting our understanding of reality in innumerable directions." (*An Introduction to Philosophy*, trans. By E.I. Watkin)

A colleague with whom I team-taught a course for thirteen years called "Athens and Jerusalem" (these cities stand for reason and faith respectively) used to make the point that the ancient Israelites had no philosophy. For example, there are no books in the Bible entitled "On the Highest Good" or "On the Ultimate Constituents of the Universe" which, of course, is true. After thinking about this for some time, I realized that one could also say that the ancient Israelites didn't have grammar in the sense that they didn't write books on the grammar of Hebrew. (Those came much later.) Nevertheless, from time immemorial as they spoke Hebrew, they followed very definite rules which were implicit in their utterances but had not yet been made explicit. So also, one could say that they didn't have philosophy in the sense that they hadn't yet written philosophical treatises, but in all of their thoughts and utterances there were implicit assumptions about what is real, what people can know, what is true, what is morally right, which conclusions follow from certain premises and which ones don't, and so forth. In other words there was an implicit philosophy in every action, thought, and assertion. I argued that, if they had made the implicit assumptions explicit, it would have been realism, "the natural philosophy of the human mind." A critic of Aristotle once said that his philosophy was "common sense rendered pedantic" which was not meant as a compliment. If, however, he had said "common sense rendered explicit," it would have been anaccurate statement in my opinion. For realists then the task of philosophers is not to invent new things but to make explicit what is implicit in our sensing, knowing, arguing, and speaking. Realism should not be covered in histories of Western thought as if it were just another -ism. It deserves special treatment. Finally, the Catholic Church has been very wise to promote the study of the philosophy of Aristotle and St. Thomas. It is without a doubt the most valuable and even most wonderful subject I ever studied.

Here are a few claims which I have argued for and am willing to defend:

- Reality comprises everything that exists including our minds. Extramental reality is exactly the same in character and structure whether we are thinking about it or knowing it or not. It would be unchanged if there were no minds.
- The cosmos existed, according to science, billions of years before *homo sapiens* evolved. If the human race were destroyed tomorrow, the universe would be no different although the environment on earth would gradually become less polluted.
- Truth is agreement or correspondence between the mind and reality. If one thinks that Canada is located immediately north of the U.S. and in fact it is, that person's belief is true. If one thinks what is is not or what is not is, that person is mistaken.
- Truth of speech consists in the agreement or correspondence between what one says to another and what one thinks. If one is convinced that two plus two equal four but tells another they equal five, that person has told a lie.
- All members of the human species share a common human nature which consists of a set of common traits. If there were no human nature, there would be no such class as homo sapiens.

- I know of no cases where, e.g. a coroner was unsure whether a body was that of a human or not, or where doctors were unsure whether an infant was human or not. This never happens because of human nature.
- Realists think that such statements as Merleau-Ponty's "It is the nature of man not to have a nature" represents a serious error.
- The cultural differences that separate members of one culture from those of other cultures are trivial compared with the underlying universal features. In *Human Universals* D.E. Brown discusses, by my estimate. ca. 400 traits found in all human cultures. Here are some examples: poetic and rhetorical speech forms, metaphors, myths, storytelling, words for days, months, seasons, years, body parts, flora, fauna, kinship categories, binary distinctions including male and female, good and bad, nature and culture, friendly greetings, crying, flirtation with the eyes, hygiene, dance, music, and on and on and on.
- Unfortunately there is a tendency to stress the differences that divide us and ignore our common humanity. Hence the popularity of talk about "diversity."
- Linguisticism is the belief that the structure of one's language determines one's view of the world. Realists think that the truth is the opposite. Language is an attempt to reflect reality.
- Morality consists of virtues which are good habits that can be developed. Most talk about "values" is nonsense.
- Philosophy is the most important subject in the liberal arts curriculum. I would advise people who wish to study philosophy on their own to begin with Mortimer Adler's *Aristotle for Everybody or Difficult Thought Made Easy.*

Theology

Meister Eckhart (1260-1327) was a Dominican theologian who taught at the University of Paris and was the most famous preacher of his day. His Latin writings have survived and are similar to those of St. Thomas Aquinas and other medieval scholars. It is his German works, however, that have earned him a place in the history of Western thought. In addition to teaching and holding numerous administrative posts in the Dominican Order, Eckhart was the spiritual director for nuns in whole regions of Germany. Since the nuns did not know Latin, he preached to them in

German, and it is in these sermons that his "mystical theology" is found, and that is what made such an impression on me. He is considered the father of German mysticism and one of the greatest of German mystics. Also, because of his arresting style and his innovative uses of German, he is counted among the founders of literary German. He was a great lover of paradoxes, as we shall see, and often, in my opinion, used unusual language and vivid images in an attempt to shock the nuns into new ways of thinking. Because of this he was frequently accused of heresy during his life, and when he died, twenty-eight of his propositions were being investigated by the then Pope, John XXII. All of these propositions were eventually judged orthodox if properly interpreted. Here are some of Eckhart's most important teachings:

Being is God. Creatures exist only as long as they receive being from God. Just as the air never possesses light—it simply receives it as long as the sun shines, and just as the mirror never has a grasp on an image—it reflects it only as long as a person or thing is in front of it, so we never have a hold on existence. Our existence is "radically contingent;" we would lapse into nothingness immediately if God were to cease sustaining us. I have found it very salutary to meditate on this proposition; it puts everything into the proper perspective.

Eckhart distinguishes between God and the Godhead. God is the deity as He is conceived of and spoken of by humans. The Godhead lies behind this and is the "naked being of God;" it is "God Himself as He is in Himself." The Godhead is prior even to the persons of the Trinity. Human language and thought are totally inadequate when it comes to speaking or thinking about the Godhead. It is hidden and is called an "abyss" and a "wasteland" since no adjectives can describe it. Furthermore, God's being is so different from the being of creatures that He can be called Non-being! This doesn't mean He doesn't exist; it's an example of Eckhart's "emphatic style" which was, as I said above, meant to shock listeners and readers into new ways of thinking. Another example of this is "If I didn't exist, God would not be God." This simply means that, if humans didn't exist, "God" as spoken of by humans would not exist (which is obvious), but, of course, the Godhead would.

The Godhead, as distinct from God is also called "the ground of God" by Eckhart. It turns out next that each human soul is "a spark," "a drop," "a small share" of divinity, and by analogy there is the soul and the "ground of the soul." The soul has its faculties, sensation, will and reason, which enables it to deal with this world. The ground of the soul, or essence of the soul, is "a hidden recess of the mind," "an inner shrine" where all is "still and silent." The ground of the soul has no contact with this world or with creatures. It exists outside of time and space. No words describe it adequately.

The ground of the soul is, in fact, one with the ground of God. It is, therefore, "timeless, eternal, pure, detached." "Where God is, there is the soul; where the soul is, there is God." The ground of the soul is the "place" among creatures into which God may come. Moreover, just as the Father gives birth to the Son in eternity, so too He gives birth to the Son in the ground of the soul if the soul is receptive. It is thus compared to Mary, and just as Mary had to give her consent ("Be it done to me according to Thy word.") so too must the soul consent. What will prevent the birth of the Son in the soul is self-love and self-will. These must be completely eradicated so one can say with St. Paul, "I live now not I, but Christ liveth in me."

According to Eckhart each of us existed as an idea in the mind of God from eternity. These ideas were our souls; so we existed before we were united with these bodies just as we hope to live after being separated from our bodies at death. Realizing this helps us understand such shocking statements of Eckhart as this: "When I still stood in my first cause, then I had no God, and there I was the cause of myself." By this he means when he was an idea in the ground of God, he had no need of "God" as humans speak of Him. Even more shocking is the following: " . . . I ask God that He may rid me of God. For my essential being is beyond God insofar as we grasp God as the beginning of creatures . . ." He wants to get rid of or go beyond God as conceived by humans, e.g. as a creator and be one with the ground of God.

John Caputo explains it as follows: "To get back to God in His innermost Godhead then means two things: it means that God ceases to be God, that is, the creator, but it also means that the soul ceases to be a creature, for it makes a regress back into its primal origin. In other words, the mystical union consists in the *undoing* of the whole creation process, in reversing its direction, in overcoming creation on both ends, so that there is neither creature nor creator." What mystics such as Eckhart seek is union with God, and for him it meant regressing to the time (before time and creation) when he was an idea in the mind of God and not a creature (and as I say this, I realize I am being inconsistent, but our language evolved to talk about things in time and space, not what is eternal and exists outside of space.)

There is another inconsistency in this chapter: in philosophy I am an Aristotelian, but Eckhart whose "mystical theology" I find so appealing was more of a Platonist! If I live long enough, I may be able to reconcile these two positions. I should mention, however, that Eckhart's mystical theology complements traditional Catholic theology; it does not replace it. (If anyone is interested in learning more about Meister Eckhart, I would recommend *The Mystical Element in Heidegger's Thought* by John Caputo. Although Eckhart is not mentioned in the title of this book, chapter three deals with him and also parts of chapters four and five. Just skip the parts that cover Heidegger. Caputo makes difficult thought comprehensible, if not easy, to paraphrase what Mortimer Adler said about Aristotle.)